Earth

Digging Deep in British Art

1781–2022

Christiana Payne
Nathalie Levi
Emma Stibbon

RWA

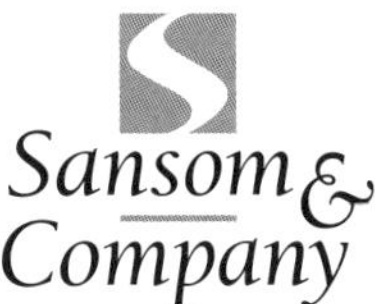

Scan the QR code on your mobile device
to access the exhibition web-page
and list of exhibited works

First published in 2022 by Sansom and Company,
a publishing imprint of Redcliffe Press Ltd.,
81G Pembroke Road, Bristol BS8 3EA
www.sansomandcompany.co.uk · info@sansomandcompany.co.uk

Published to coincide with the exhibition
'Earth: Digging Deep In British Art 1781–2022',
Royal West of England Academy (RWA), Bristol, 9 July–11 September 2022,
an original exhibition conceived by Nathalie Levi.

The exhibition has been made possible as a result of the Government Indemnity Scheme.The RWA would like to thank HM Government for providing Government Indemnity and the Department for Digital, Culture, Media and Sport and Arts Council England for arranging the indemnity.

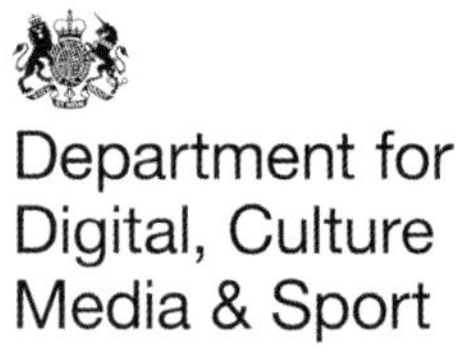

ISBN 978-1-911408-92-5
British Library cataloguing-in-publication data:
a catalogue record for this book is available from the British Library.

Edited by Ann Kay and Nathalie Levi
Printed and bound by Cambrian Press

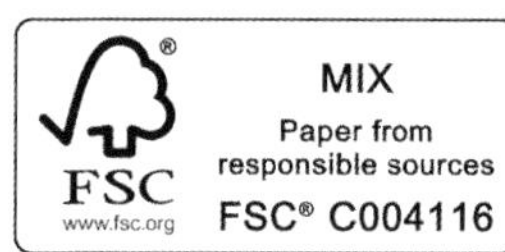

This book is made from Forest Stewardship Council® certified paper.
Sansom & Co is committed to being an environmentally friendly publisher.

Front cover · Graham Sutherland OM · 1903–1980
Cornish Tin Mine, Emerging Miner
1943 · oil on canvas · 118.1 x 76.2 cm

Contents

Foreword

The word 'earth' conveys a multitude of meanings. It is the planet on which we all live; the soil that gives nourishment to our crops; an essential conduit making electricity safe; a dwelling or hiding place for wildlife, and the ground beneath our feet and into which we will ultimately be subsumed.

More than anything earth is associated with solidity, yet its vulnerability is becoming all too apparent. As we all become increasingly conscious of the climate emergency, it seems apt to present this exhibition celebrating, exploring and conceptualising the theme of earth.

Like all RWA exhibitions, we hope that everyone will find something to love in this show, no matter what your taste, background or state of mind - something to uplift the spirit; provoke a poignant memory; inspire your own creativity; feel connected to artists of the past and present: something to nourish your soul.

We also hope that this show will be the catalyst and forum for debate about the single biggest issue facing humanity: the fragility of our planet and the urgent need to address climate change. I urge everyone to think about their own ecological footprint, and if in a position to do so, be a part of effecting positive change, large or small.

We are hugely grateful to all those who have enabled us to stage this exhibition and accompanying activity programme, which have been made possible through an Arts Council National Lottery Project Grant.

We are particularly indebted to Emma Stibbon RA RWA, Professor Emerita Christiana Payne and Nathalie Levi for their brilliant curation of the show and insightful contributions to this publication.

We also thank all the artists who have brought their breadth of vision to bear, and all of the lenders, public and private, who have enabled us to share masterpieces from the past with the public here in Bristol.

Every RWA exhibition and project is a testament to our fantastic team of staff, freelancers and volunteers. We are particularly proud that, through the hard work and dedication of Helen Jacobs and our Learning & Engagement team, creative activities will take place across the city and will include people with extreme wellbeing challenges, as well as our wide and growing RWA community.

Finally, we thank all our supporters, from those who purchase a ticket or an art pass to our Patrons, Friends, sponsors and benefactors: we couldn't survive without you.

Alison Bevan
RWA Director

Introduction

'Earth: Digging Deep in British Art 1781–2022' is the final instalment of the RWA's element-themed exhibition series, following 'The Power of the Sea: Making Waves in British Art 1790–2014' (2014), 'Air: Visualising the Invisible in British Art 1768–2017' (2017) and 'Fire: Flashes to Ashes in British Art 1692–2019' (2019). It tackles the most expansive and urgent of subject matters, bringing together historical and contemporary artworks.

For as long as we have walked the earth, it has provided an endless source of inspiration for artists striving to capture nature's majesty. Vertiginous mountainsides and contemplative coastal scenes join panoramic views of our local landscape. The Avon Gorge, Bristol is the starting point for Emma Stibbon's essay 'Muddy Waters', taking in Richard Long's mudworks, Samuel Jackson's watercolours and her own visceral connection to the environment around the Avon.

Artists' timeless connection to the very 'stuff' of the earth is explored in my essay. This traces a line from our earliest art materials – including paints made with peat – to artists Anya Gallaccio and Andrew Hardwick incorporating earth itself as a material into their artwork. It then considers the current and future effects of human impact on the earth. As cliffsides collapse and coasts erode, contemporary artists including Yinka Shonibare, Julian Perry and Alice Cunningham investigate reactions to the climate, natural disasters and the effects of unsustainable pressure on our planet's resources.

Once seen as signs of great progress, mining, quarrying and industry brought some dark, exploitative practices against which perceptions started to shift in the twentieth century – as seen in work by Graham Sutherland. In contrast, the earth has been recognised historically as the ultimate provider. Harvest scenes and depictions of fruit, flowers and vegetables by Stanley Spencer, William Henry Hunt and John Constable delight in the bountifulness of the 'good earth', as Christiana Payne explores in her essay.

An appreciation for the natural world has grown in the wake of the global Covid pandemic, when the link between our own well-being and nature has been felt more acutely. While access to green spaces has become more important to us all, it remains unavailable for many, prompting questions of physical and cultural boundaries. In earlier centuries, too, ownership of, and access to, land was hotly disputed, and artists recorded the changing landscape of common lands and enclosures, with or without implied comment.

This exhibition goes deep beneath the earth, exposes the core materiality of its elements, explores the substance of the surface, climbs dizzying heights and perches perilously on its edges. It bears witness to the earth's mistreatment and its magnificence, its fullness and its fragility. 'Earth' surveys the representation of our environment across four centuries, inviting us to consider our planet in all its abundance, precarity and preciousness.

Nathalie Levi
Head of Programme – Curator of Exhibitions
Royal West of England Academy (RWA)

The bountiful earth

Christiana Payne

What do we mean when we write, speak or think about earth, or the Earth? Do we envisage the whole planet – the bedrock that surrounds the molten core – or the soil in which our food is grown? Do we think about harvests and gardens, or about mountains, earthquakes and catastrophes? All these themes, and more, have exercised the artists represented in this exhibition.

As this is the last in a series of four exhibitions at the RWA, the others focusing on sea, air and fire, we might start with the concept of earth in traditional thinking about the four elements. In 1586 the Dutch artist Hendrick Goltzius produced illustrations of Earth, Air, Fire and Water. Earth (fig. 1) was personified as a nude woman, with ears of wheat and flowers in her hair, clutching a cornucopia (a horn of plenty) overflowing with fruits, vegetables and leaves. In the background on the right we see the creation of Adam, the first human being: he arises from out of a rocky soil, his feet and legs still embedded in it as he rises up and takes in his new environment. Trees and animals surround him. The nude woman stands on a rock, representing the solid matter composing so much of the globe, often hidden below soil and grass, but exposed on mountains and coasts.

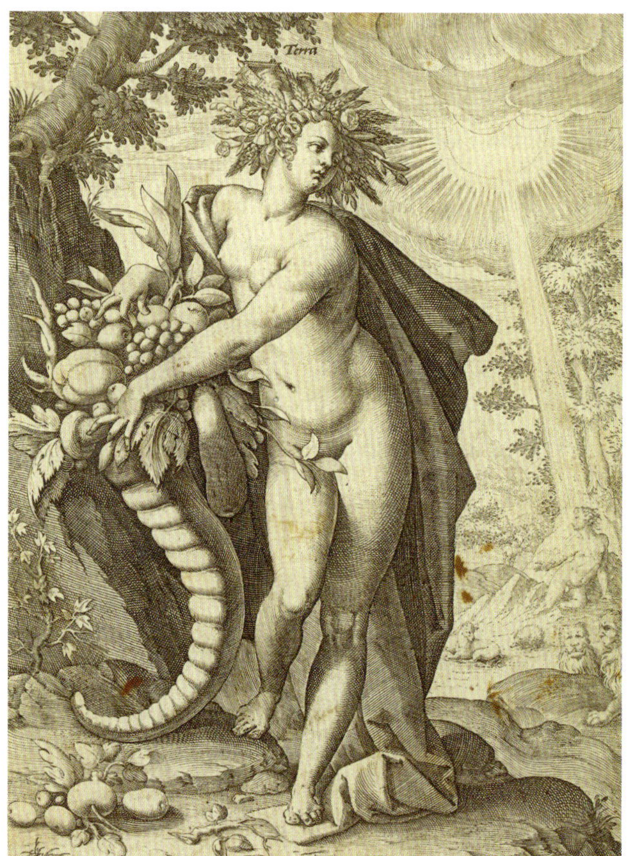

FIG. 1 · **after Hendrick Goltzius** · ***The Four Elements: Earth***
1586 · engraving on paper · 21.6 x 15.8 cm
British Museum · © The Trustees of the British Museum

Visual depictions of the elements were popular in art from the Middle Ages to the eighteenth century, and Earth is always shown as a source of sustenance and abundance. The idea of the earth as bountiful goes back to classical times and beyond. Usually gendered as female ('Mother Earth'), she appears as an earth goddess in many religions. Cybele was worshipped as the great mother of the gods in Asia Minor. For the Romans, Ceres was the goddess of

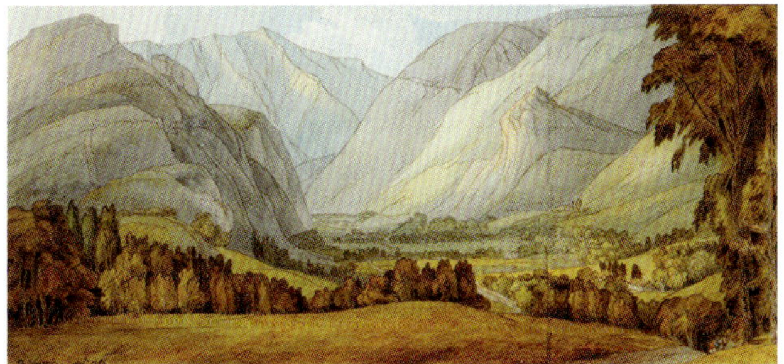

FIG. 2 · **Francis Towne** · **bap. 1739-1816**
A View taken in The Vale of St John
1786 · watercolour with pen and ink on paper · 15.6 x 33.7 cm
Leeds Museums and Galleries: bequeathed by Agnes and Norman Lupton, 1952

harvest, especially the grain harvest, while Bacchus was the god of wine and hence of the grape harvest. All three appear together in a painting of *Earth* by Francesco Albani (1625; Galleria Sabauda, Turin), along with Flora, goddess of flowers and of the spring. Earth was associated with growth, nature and agricultural activities. According to Michael Philipp, who has made a study of these allegorical representations, 'Earth was symbolised by plants, fruit, fields of grain, spades, ploughs, sickles, forests, wreaths of flowers, or the globe.'[1] By the late seventeenth century, the scientists no longer believed that there were only four elements (the current total stands at 118), but the idea of the bountiful earth continued to inspire artists to celebrate its productiveness.

Contemporary artists, on the other hand, are particularly keen on exploring the materiality of earth, recognising that for centuries artists have literally used the earth to paint, with pigments and chalks drawn from different types of rock. Artists have long been inspired by the hard underlying structure of the planet, as well as what grows on its topsoil. In the late eighteenth century the taste for 'the sublime' sent many British artists, including Francis Towne (fig. 2 and p. 25), Thomas Gainsborough (p. 27) and Philip James de Loutherbourg (p. 29), off to the Alps and the Lake District to explore the immensity and solitude of the mountains. Advances in the science of geology encouraged others, such as John Sell Cotman (p. 37) and Edward Cooke (p. 51) in the early to mid-nineteenth century, to study rock formations. These were particularly visible around the coast, where the different strata could be clearly discerned. Moreover, the instability of the coast could lead to sublime effects, such as the landslip near Lyme Regis in 1839, the aftermath of which was recorded on the spot by Mary Buckland (p. 47). Similarly, artists have enjoyed painting the exposure and penetration of the earth by mining operations: terrifying and awe-inspiring in the work of Graham Sutherland (fig. 18 and p. 65), sources of appealing light and colour in that of Laura Knight (p. 55) and Samuel John Lamorna Birch (p. 59).

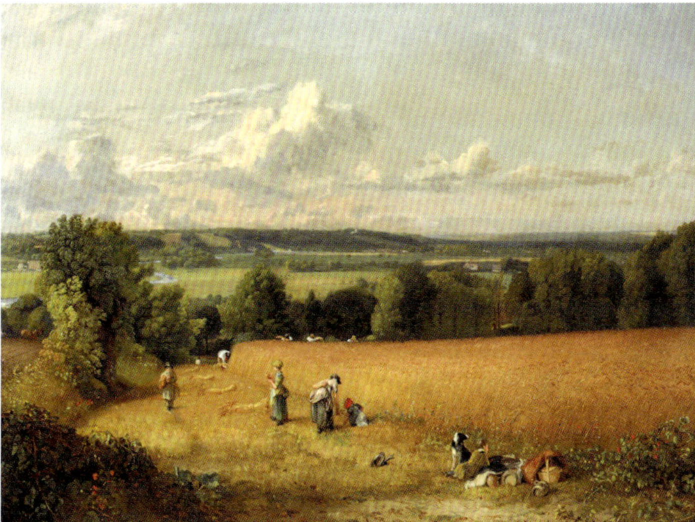

FIG. 3 · **John Constable RA** · **1776-1837** · ***The Wheat Field***
1816 · oil on canvas · 54.6 x 78.1 cm
gift of the Manton Art Foundation in memory of Sir Edwin and Lady Manton, 2007 · The Clark Art Institute (2007.8.27) · image courtesy Clark Art Institute (clarkart.edu)

Alongside the excitements of the sublime, British artists of the eighteenth and nineteenth centuries continued to depict

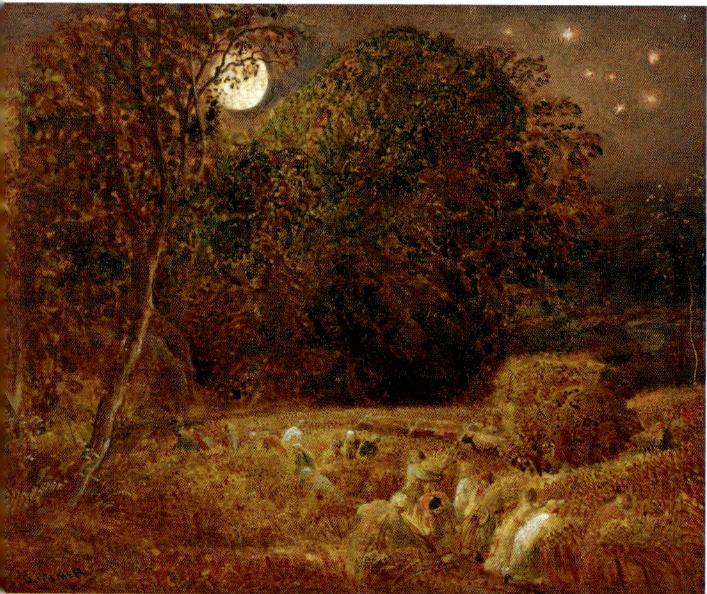

FIG. 4 · **Samuel Palmer RWS Hon. RE** · **1805-1881** · ***The Harvest Moon***
*c.*1833 · oil on paper laid on panel · 22.2 x 27.6 cm
Yale Center for British Art, Paul Mellon Collection

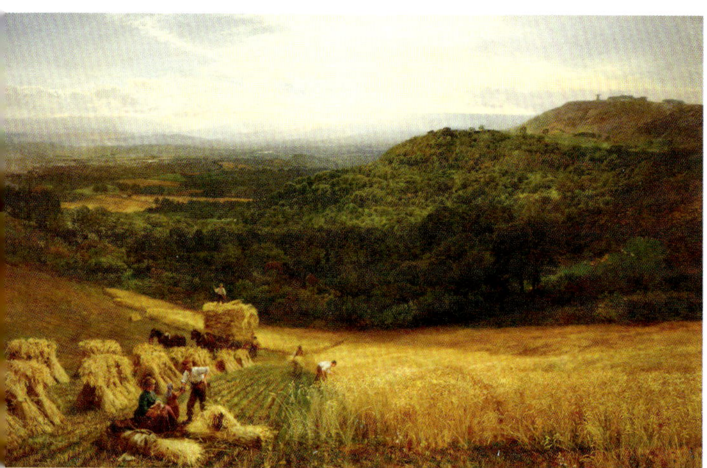

FIG. 5 · **George Vicat Cole RA** · **1833-1893** · ***Harvest Time***
1860 · oil on canvas · 94.6 x 151 cm
purchased with the assistance of the Victoria and Albert Museum Purchase Grant Fund and the Friends of Bristol Art Gallery, 1982 · Bristol Culture: Bristol Museum and Art Gallery

scenes of abundance and celebration. Landowners, commissioning views of their country estates, liked the artists to include evidence of their good husbandry in the form of fields full of waving corn and well-fed livestock. Even J.M.W. Turner, whose work is more usually sublime rather than pastoral, began a harvest scene in the early 1800s, probably 1809. This was a year in which the home production of wheat was particularly important, because Napoleon's blockade of the Channel ports was preventing imports from coming into the country. Turner's unfinished painting, *Cassiobury Park: Reaping* (p. 31), documents the estate of the 5th Earl of Essex; around 15 years later another artist, the watercolourist William Henry Hunt, recorded the excellence of the products of the same landowner's hothouses in his portrait of the estate's head gardener (p. 43). Several artists marked the final years of the Napoleonic Wars, 1814 and 1815, with paintings of golden wheat harvests. John Constable, who had a thorough understanding of agriculture, wrote in August 1815 that he was living wholly in his father's fields and seeing nobody but the harvest men.[2] In this summer, the year of Napoleon's final defeat at the Battle of Waterloo in June, Constable painted a *Wheat Field* (fig. 3) and two careful studies of his father's gardens. The subject matter of *Golding Constable's Kitchen Garden* (p. 33) combines the productiveness of horticulture with that of agriculture. The vegetable garden, with its rich brown earth, sets off the golden colours of the ripe corn in the fields beyond. Such images celebrated the peace and plenty that, it was hoped, would follow the long years of war.

In the 1820s a group of artists around the poet-painter William Blake took up the theme of pastoral contentment in a different way, interpreting it with an emphasis on internal vision and imagination and a sense of the value of the primitive. Blake's illustrations to the works of an imitator of the Roman poet Virgil (p. 35) were the catalyst for the 'Shoreham Period' work of Samuel Palmer and his friends, who called themselves 'the Ancients' and gathered to read poetry and go for moonlit walks in the village of Shoreham in Kent. Wheat harvests were prominent again: wheat was the 'staff of life' at a time when many of the poorer people in the country ate little else. The Ancients also had a special fondness for the cider produced in the region, and derived, of course, from apples. Palmer painted harvesters working far into the night by the light of a huge harvest moon (fig. 4). His close friend Edward Calvert depicted a more pagan, bacchanalian scene of revellers dancing in front of an even larger moon as the abundant apple harvest is crushed and pressed to make cider (p. 45). In these works the productiveness of the earth was seen as proof of the goodness of a benevolent God. Their self-consciously primitive style is intended to refer both to the visionary nature of their imaginings and to the humility with which the artists felt they should express themselves. Palmer's 'Shoreham Period' lasted for a relatively short time, but he continued to produce scenes celebrating the abundance of the earth, depicting the grape harvests of Italy (p. 49) as well as the corn harvests of southern England.

Painted harvest scenes were popular again in the 1850s and 1860s, the so-called 'golden age' of British agriculture. Artists such as George Vicat Cole were able to make a good living specialising in such works, which combined careful open-air study with an emphasis on happy family groups that made them very appealing to purchasers. Vicat Cole, we are told, painted his cheerful harvest scenes from a hut on Holmbury Hill in Surrey. The local farmers 'would leave in the fields patches of corn uncut, stooks uncarted, and waggons ready-loaded, until the artist had finished what he wanted of them'.[3] His painting *Harvest Time* (fig. 5) incorporates a view over a vast expanse of country, the golden fields in the foreground contrasting with the deep green of the woods beyond – a vision of a healthy, fertile and peaceful land. In reality, the British countryside was not a place of unalloyed peace and plenty. The enclosure of the common fields in the earlier part of the century had left many agricultural labourers desperately poor, and farm work, in the days before mechanisation, was grindingly hard, and often monotonous. George Clausen's *Winter Work* (p. 53) gives a powerful impression of the other side of the labourer's life, complete with thick mud, inadequate clothing and frozen hands. This kind of picture was not so successful with buyers and critics, who preferred not to be reminded of such evident signs of poverty and distress.

More distressing scenes appear in the war paintings of the brothers Paul and John Nash (p. 57). These make it clear that the trench warfare of the First World War (1914–18) was an environmental as well as a human tragedy. Their studies and paintings show the bare earth exposed and parched, the trees dead or dying, like the soldiers. One of Paul Nash's most powerful statements of the theme has the ironic title *We Are Making a New World* (fig. 6). It becomes ever more relevant now, as we realise that we cannot make a new world: there is no planet B, this is the only one we have and we need to look after it. The land can regenerate, as the fields of Normandy did after the war, but this will not go on forever. These paintings now seem like a prescient anticipation of our own concerns with pollution, soil erosion and climate change.

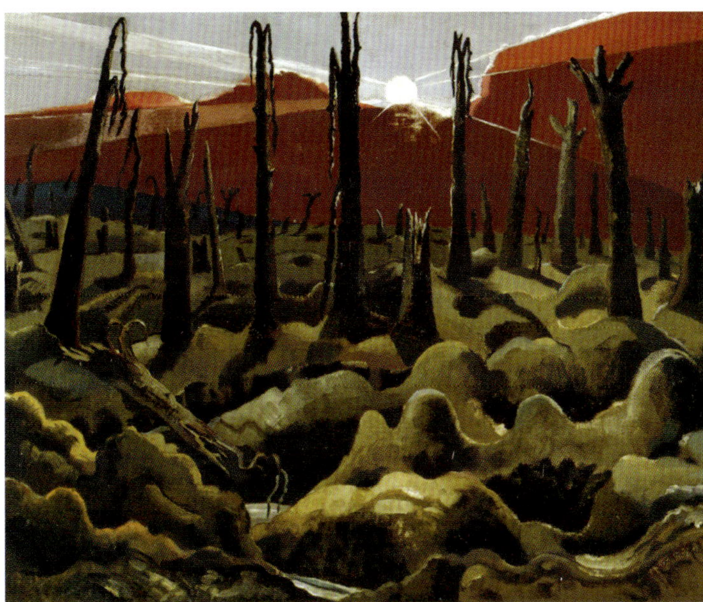

FIG. 6 · **Paul Nash** · 1889–1946 · ***We Are Making a New World***
1918 · oil on canvas · 71.1 x 91.4 cm
Imperial War Museum · © IWM (Art.IWM ART 1146)

On a more optimistic note, the tradition of Palmer and Constable was revived in the 1930s in the landscapes of Stanley Spencer. Like these earlier artists, Spencer was attached to a particular place, in his case the village of Cookham in Berkshire. In his figure paintings, this village is the scene of miracles and resurrections. In his landscapes, there is always profusion and abundance: of flowers, shrubs and trees, of fruit and vegetables, and of animal life. He professed to be irritated that collectors preferred these works to his religious paintings, but the loving detail with which the everyday elements are recorded tells a different story. He seems to be entranced by the contrasts in colour and texture of objects that other artists might have considered beneath their notice: corrugated iron roofs (p. 63) or huge onions (fig. 7). In these paintings the produce of the earth takes on the aura of the miraculous.

Traditional ideas of the bountiful earth and the modern emphasis on materiality come together in watercolours by Eric Ravilious and John Nash. Compared to the exuberant landscapes of Spencer, they may seem rather bleak, with their large areas of bare soil. However, this is the soil that will bear the harvests of the future. Nash's ploughed field (p. 69) is ready for the seed drill, while Ravilious's (p. 61) has already been sown, as the presence of the roller attests. All these artists celebrate the earth as the source of food, as well as a source of mental, spiritual and emotional well-being. Their depictions can help us to become more aware of our dependence on a healthy planet. We do not need to believe it is proof of a divine Creator in order to be grateful for it, and to understand how important it is that we do our best to preserve its beauty and its productiveness for generations yet unborn.

1. Michael Philipp, 'The Whole and Its Parts: Visual Depictions of the Four Elements from the Middle Ages to the Eighteenth Century', in Ortrud Westheider and Michael Philipp (eds), *Turner and the Elements* (Munich: Hirmer Verlag, 2011), p. 25.
2. R.B. Beckett (ed.), *John Constable's Correspondence* (Ipswich: Suffolk Records Society, 1962–9), vol. II, p. 149 (letter to his future wife Maria Bicknell, 27 August 1815).
3. R. Chignell, *The Life and Paintings of George Vicat Cole* (London: 1898), vol. I, pp. 68, 10.

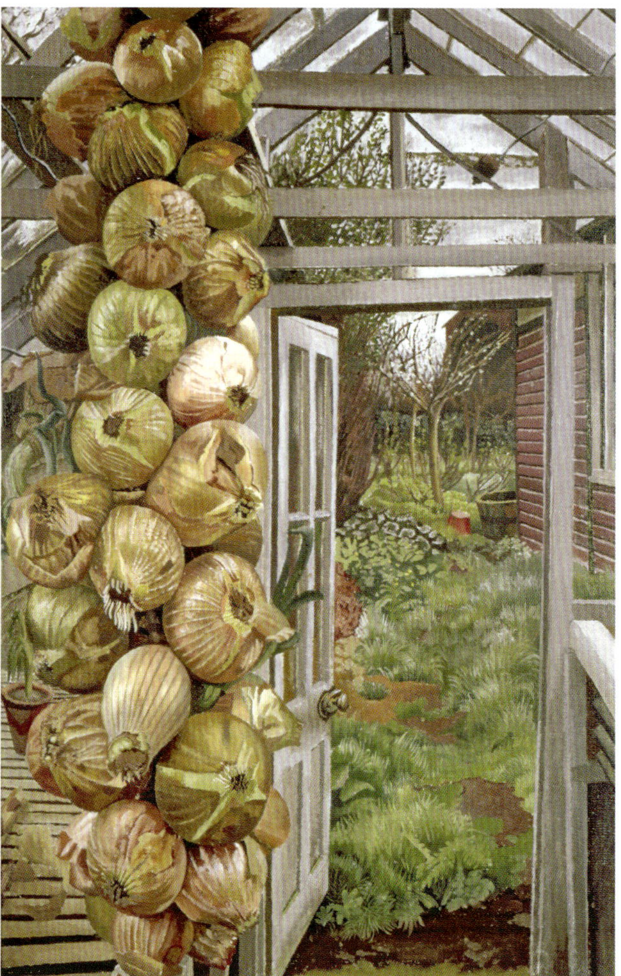

FIG. 7 · **Stanley Spencer CBE RA** · **1891–1959** · ***Greenhouse and Garden***
1937 · oil on canvas · 76.2 x 50.8 cm
Ferens Art Gallery, Hull Museums · © Ferens Art Gallery

The earth's the limit

Nathalie Levi

'This is the place where I found the red stone. I've found this red all over the world, in every country that I've worked in, and the reason blood is red is because of its iron content, so we share a connection with the stone. When I find it in Australia or Japan or France, I feel like I'm touching a bit of the red here too, and tapping into the same vein'[1]

Andy Goldsworthy

In every area where prehistoric sites have been discovered, miles of trails lead to hematite mines, a then highly coveted form of iron oxide found in the Earth's shallow crust. It is one of the earliest durable pigments, its colour an earthy red. Over a million years ago, archaic peoples walked long distances in search of it.[2] The need to create a lasting mark was the motivation behind the first known mining activity. Driven perhaps by artistic endeavour, perhaps to indicate territory or to tell stories, people began to dig.

'Earth: Digging Deep in British Art 1781–2022' does not go quite so far back in history, though many of the artists included in the exhibition and this book evoke the timeless connection between art and earth compounds. Right up until the invention of modern artificial pigments in the nineteenth century, essentially paint was made by grinding down earth and mineral compounds into fine powder. Our prehistoric ancestors crushed hematite and mixed it with vegetable oil as a very early precursor to oil paint. Little changed until around 3,000 years ago, when the Egyptians and Chinese developed ways of washing earth pigments to improve their potency, and produced them on a large scale. They dedicated more time and effort to making artists' colours than any other civilization would for thousands of years. A renewal in interest came with the artistic and technological advances of the Renaissance in the fifteenth century. Sienna and umber pigments were roasted to make deeper, richer reds and earth colours were used routinely in painting techniques, even for flesh tones, which were underpainted in Terre Verte (green earth).

One particular pigment, called Cassel Earth, was originally made from peat and unsurprisingly found to be especially useful for landscapes. Although Peter Paul Rubens (fig. 8) and his student Anthony van Dyck are known more for their figurative work, the pigment was so favoured by them that the colour later went by their names, as Rubens or Vandyke Brown. Thomas Gainsborough (p. 27), who was greatly inspired by van Dyck, was also known to use it abundantly in his work.

Using earth elements in pigments has long enriched and enabled the creation of artworks, functioning as the painter's primary tool for attaining a particular colour or tone, evoking a mood, creating contrast, varnishing or sealing a work. Paints have become more sophisticated and synthetic over the centuries, and today pretty much anything can be used to make art, but the impetus to draw on the environment around us remains. There is a continuing allegiance to natural materials, the very 'stuff' of the earth, throughout contemporary art. For example, Emma Stibbon, Fiona Hingston and Andrew Hardwick, in their individual approaches to landscape practice, all incorporate physical parts of their surroundings into their depictions of it. Stibbon's impulse is to respond to a period of unprecedented change, embarking on long journeys of her own, from arctic glaciers to Hawaiian islands. In her *Broken Terrain* print, she scattered volcanic ash gathered from the Big Island into her drawing ink. It depicts the volatility of a landscape that experiences thousands of earthquakes a year (p. 121). Stibbon's journeying is a way of working that is rooted in Western landscape art and undeniably borrows from its 'sublime' tradition, but is framed by a climate-conscious outlook.

For Hardwick, it is the soil and substrate of the expansive area near the mouth of the River Avon, where his family has lived and farmed for generations, that is layered into heavily textured paintings (p. 89). Hingston's *Field Walking* series (p. 93), meanwhile, focuses in on ploughed fields, working earth into ink. Both these artists have deep, personal ties to the landscapes they describe in their artwork, landscapes they have seen shift in form and use over the course of their lifetimes. Ploughing, for example, may soon be a thing of the past, regarded as an unsustainable method of farming. Up until the 1930s, however, the theory that 'rain follows the plow'[3] was widely held as an early form of climate science. It was believed that ploughing could quite literally make it rain. Though this idea is long discredited, in our environmentally enlightened times we are all too aware of the impact of human activity on the climate. There has been a worldwide awakening, but unless our lives are fundamentally affected by climate change - as they are in many places around the world already suffering its devastating effects - it remains something that exists in the abstract.

Visualising climate change was a challenge taken on by artist Alice Cunningham while on a residency at the University of Bristol's Earth Sciences department. Working with climate scientists, Cunningham developed a series of stone sculptures using rocks from the Earth Sciences archive, some dating back to the Triassic period, under the title *What Does Climate Change Look Like?* (fig. 9). They are delicately carved, precariously balanced, artistic interpretations of the fractures and lines on geological surfaces that are analysed in scientific study.

Taking an incredibly broad view of climate change is Siobhán McDonald's *A History of Time* series (p. 103). In this impressive

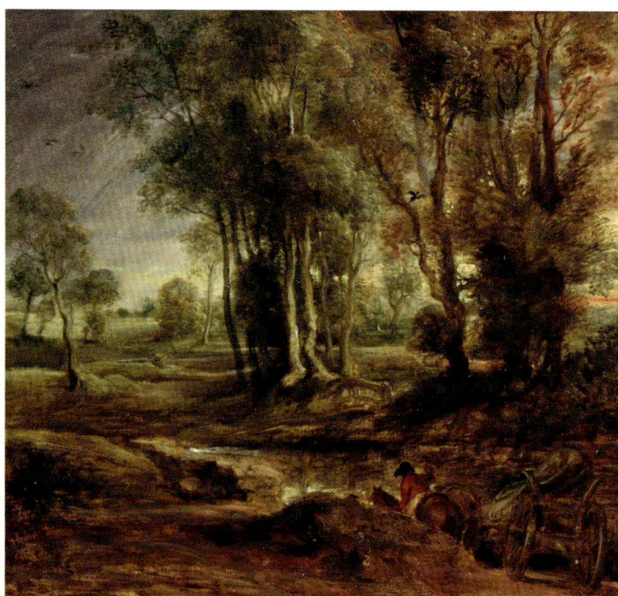

FIG. 8 · **Peter Paul Rubens** · **1577-1640**
Evening landscape with timber wagon
1630-40 · oil on panel · 49.5 x 54.7 cm
Collection Museum Boijmans Van Beuningen, Rotterdam · acquired with the collection of D.G. Van Beuningen, 1958 (former collection Koenigs) photographer: Studio Tromp

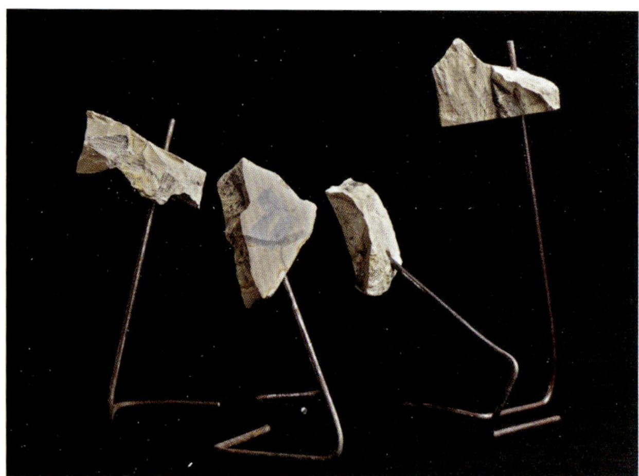

FIG. 9 · **Alice Cunningham MRSS** · **b.1983**
What Does Climate Change Look Like?
2018 · landscape marble · various dimensions
courtesy and © the artist

project, ghostly photogenic images of the planet's earliest plant life were developed in a photographic darkroom in the atmospheric chambers of the Programme for Experimental Atmospheres and Climate (PÉAC). McDonald used fossilised leaves, silver nitrate and light to create prints generated by a 400-million-year-old atmosphere – an atmosphere so deadly that two inhalations could kill you. A stark warning for us today. McDonald collaborated with scientist Professor Jennifer McElwain, Chair of Botany, Trinity College Dublin, who uses fossilised plants to reconstruct the evolution of Earth's climate conditions and investigate global warming events that took place millions of years ago.

Over the past few decades artists have been increasingly exploring our climate crisis in their work. For some it is in referential ways that combine art with scientific processes, such as Cunningham and McDonald. For others it is a more direct confrontation, such as Yinka Shonibare's *Earth Kids* (p. 119), which are, in the artist's own words, 'a call to action to protect the planet for our children'. Shonibare's child-size figures have heat-map globes for heads and wear Victorian-style clothing printed with Dutch wax patterns, linking colonial exploitation with the exploitation of our planet's natural resources. They are symbolic of the messages being championed by child activists. Recent years have seen young people lead the way in calling for greater climate consciousness: school strikes, marches and youth movements demanding that policy-makers, and all adults, take heed and do more to reduce emissions and impact on the environment, while there is still time to enact change.

Growing numbers of activists and artists seek to remind us of our primordial connection with the earth that has dissipated over the centuries. Increasingly urban lifestyles have distanced people from nature, and access to it is a privilege that not all are able to enjoy – urban green space in England declined by eight per cent between 2001 and 2018.[4] Despite its eco-friendly credentials, Bristol has one of England's largest areas of urban sprawl, to the north of the city. The M32 and M4 cut through prime agricultural land that used to be the city's historic market-garden quarter. Here there is still dark red nutrient-rich growing soil that campaigning organisations such as the Blue Finger Alliance are trying to protect. Up and down the country, vast areas of what was once farmland and wildlife habitat have become secondary spaces. Drawing our attention to them is Carol Rhodes in her contemplative bird's-eye-view paintings of out-of-town office complexes, airports, factories, service stations and road networks (p. 117), and Edward Chell in his series of paintings *The Garden of England* (p. 79). Chell takes the UK's motorway verges as subject matter. They have been called Britain's 'largest unofficial nature reserve' and one that next to no one has visited, though we have all probably passed through.

Addressing our disconnection from the environment is the focus of Dalziel + Scullion's art, which offers methods that re-establish a more reflective and profound connection with nature. Their practical handbook, *Homing*, is a manual 'to rekindle our abilities to find our way back "home" to an organic world of plants and animals, land and sea, weather and seasons'.[5] In *Immersion Clothing* (p. 83), a series of garments invites the wearer to behave differently, to slow down and shift perceptions, to re-engage with what has become habitual and matter of fact. Immersing you in, rather than protecting you from, the elements. They include a hooded jacket that changes the familiar shape of the human silhouette, while another has pockets tailored for collecting botanical and geological finds, rather than mobile phones and wallets.

While we could all benefit from switching off and tuning in to the natural world more, someone who became intensely connected to a rural area is sculptor Kabir Hussain. He spent a year on a residency at White House Farm, Great Glemham, in the Alde Valley in Suffolk, becoming intimately acquainted with the lifecycle of the land while undertaking a study of a sugar-beet field. Like Samuel Palmer, John Constable and Stanley Spencer before him, Hussain continues the traditions of finding the revelatory in nature. He spoke of the field having a life of its own, of the power of the natural forces at work and the terrifying moment the beets burst from the ground, describing them as 'giant beasts'. He later cast several of the beasts in bronze, paying tribute to their awesome force (fig. 11). His work captures the energy in the earth in a way that complements rather than controls, and fosters a respectful relationship with the produce of our land, reimagined in the same material we use for our monuments.

Bronze casting is a highly skilled process but it can be unpredictable, particularly when unusual organic materials are involved. Some beets cracked open the plaster (used to encase them in a casting mould), as though trying to escape once again. An element of unpredictability is something that artists like Andy Goldsworthy and Anya Gallaccio have embraced, stepping back and allowing natural materials to lead in the creation of the artwork. In his series of *Snowball Drawings* (eg. fig. 10), Goldsworthy simply allows a snowball to melt on watercolour paper: *Source of Scaur*, for example, combines crushed red stone and natural materials collected from the River Scaur into the ice, leaving an imprint in that familiar earthy, iron-rich red. Anya Gallaccio's dirt drawings, meanwhile, follow traditional paper marbling techniques using earth and sand collected during a road trip through deserts in south-western US states. The aesthetically pleasing results are mostly down to chance (p. 87).

David Nash's *Wooden Boulder* (p. 105) is another remarkable example of physically 'letting go' and allowing natural forces to run their own course in art. After carving a rough sphere from a fallen tree in North Wales in 1978, Nash rolled it into a stream and has followed its movements ever since. Sculpted as much by the elements as by human hand, the boulder continues to appear and disappear in the local landscape, coming and going with the tides and changing seasons, and was last sighted seven years ago.

These philosophical pieces quietly invoke thoughts of our place in the world. They could be seen as poetic lessons in losing control, and finding beauty in doing so. There is an innate respect for the natural materials themselves. They are not just functional here – serving only to manifest an artist's vision – but are co-authors of the artwork. With the lightness of touch, you'd be forgiven for thinking the results are purely incidental. They speak instead of how the slightest of actions can set off a chain of events, take on its own meaning, and become symbolic of a more sensitive, reciprocal relationship with our environment.

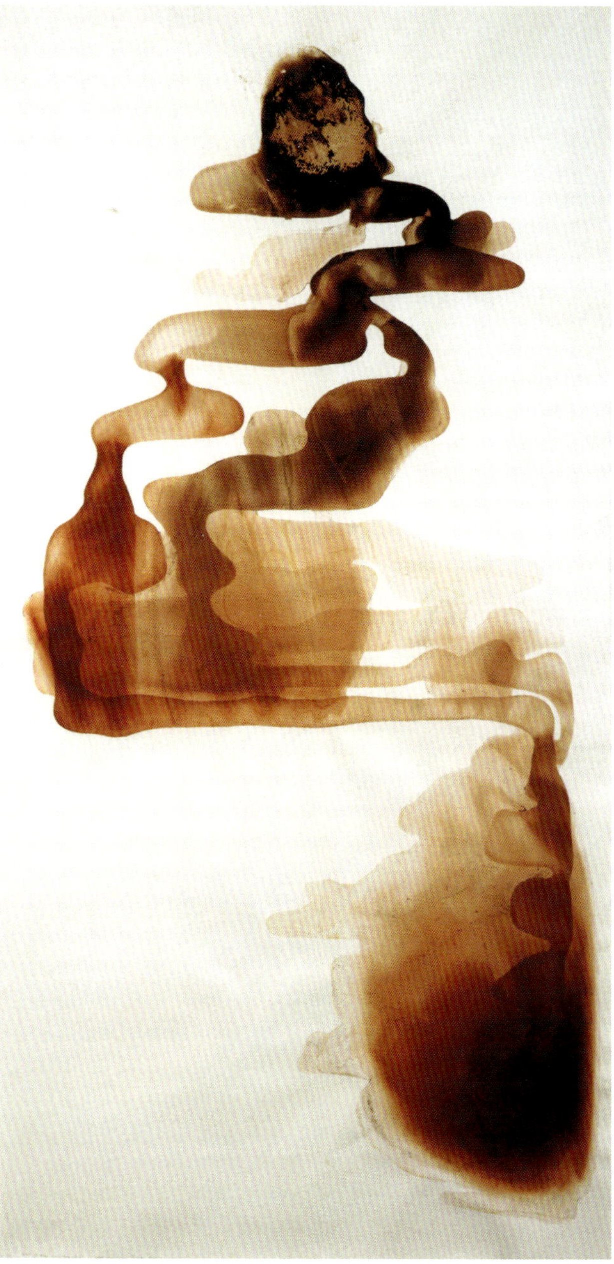

FIG. 10 · **Andy Goldsworthy OBE** · **b.1956** · ***Source of Scaur***
1991–2 · melted snowball and stone on paper · 235 x 121 cm
Victoria and Albert Museum, London · © Andy Goldsworthy courtesy Galerie Lelong & Co., New York

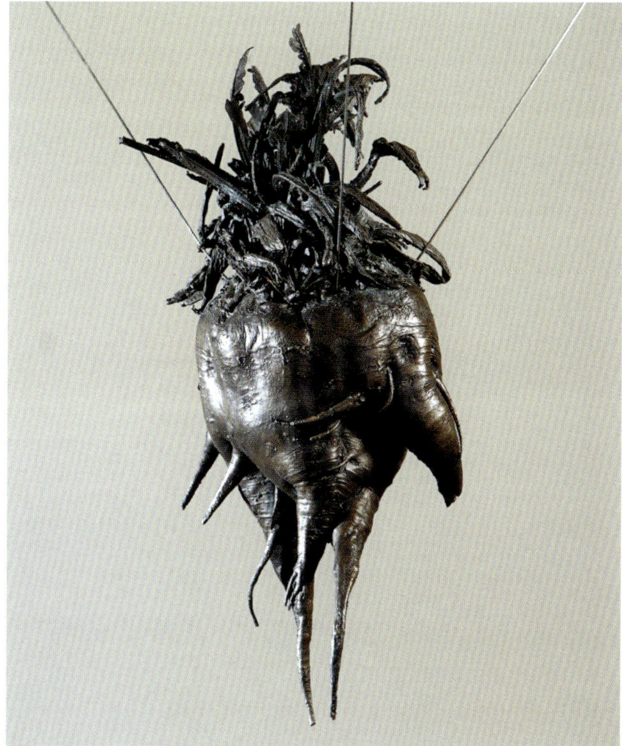

FIG. 11 · **Kabir Hussain** · **b.1960** · ***Stingray Sugar Beet***
2017 · bronze · 51 x 24 cm
courtesy and © the artist · photograph Jonathan Callery

Our ancestors couldn't possibly have comprehended the dawn of art, culture and civilisation that would follow from their discovery of this humble rock as they travelled far on foot to find it. For as long as humans are here on this planet, there will be the mark-makers, those who will go the extra mile to tell our stories. It is up to us, in the here and now, to protect the resources we know aren't limitless, and ensure there will be many more stories to tell.

1. Andy Goldsworthy, 'We Share a Connection with Stone', TateShots, 1 December 2011, on www.youtube.com and at www.tate.org.uk/art/artists/andy-goldsworthy-7274/andy-goldsworthy-share-connection-stone.
2. E. Pernicka and G. Weisgerber, 'Ore Mining in Prehistoric Europe: An Overview', in G. Morteani and J.P. Northover (eds), *Prehistoric Gold in Europe: Mines, Metallurgy and Manufacture* (Dordrecht, Boston, London: Springer, 1995), pp. 159–82.
3. H.N. Smith, 'Rain Follows the Plow: The Notion of Increased Rainfall for the Great Plains, 1844–1880', *Huntington Library Quarterly*, vol. 10, no. 2 (February 1947), pp. 169–93.
4. Public Health England, *Improving Access to Greenspace: A New Review for 2020* (London: PHE Publications, March 2020).
5. M. Dalziel and L. Scullion, *Homing* (Dunbar: North Lights Arts, 2018).
6. I. Pollard, *Postcards Home* (London: Chris Boot, 2005).

We can only speculate as to what first motivated our ancestors to dig deep in search of pigment, what it must have been like to discover it. But until a few years ago you could still visit a hematite mine here in the UK: the Florence Iron mine in Cumbria (closed in 2007). Photographer Ingrid Pollard wrote about a trip she made there in her monograph *Postcards Home*, describing it as 'all red walls and the darkest, blackest, lightless place'.[6] The visit must have left an impression as a piece of hematite, presumably from this visit, features in Pollard's *Bursting Stone* series, exploring the geologies and industries of the Lake District as a counterpoint to its quaint touristic image. Interestingly, the photographs that are included in this body of work are all monochrome, the hematite rock standing out as a flash of sudden colour.

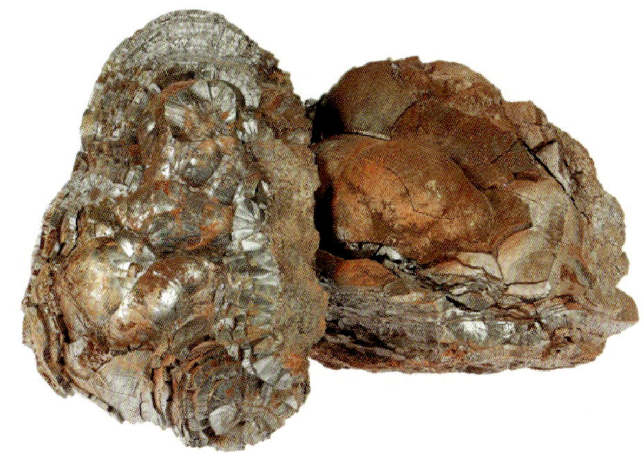

FIG. 12 · **Hematite (kidney ore) from Florence Mine, Egremont, England**
Björn Wylezich/Alamy Stock Photo

Muddy waters

Emma Stibbon RA RWA

On my daily walk to the studio I cross the Cut, a brown waterway that diverts the River Avon through south Bristol. The tidal reach scours the riverbed, redepositing its fine clay into delicate rills and mudbanks outside my studio at Spike Island. I look out onto this primal scene and feel connected to the muddy flow and life of the river (fig. 12).

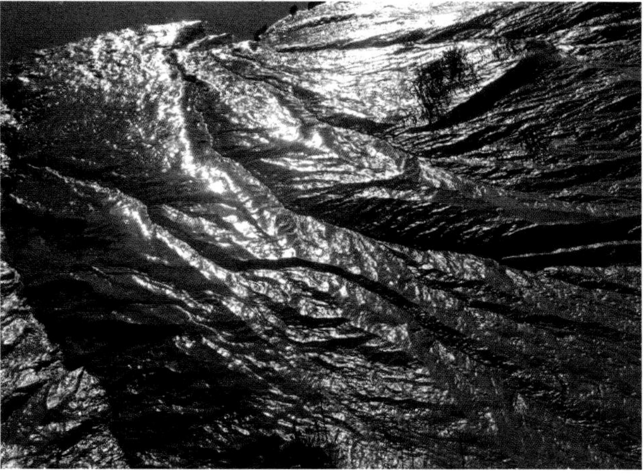

FIG. 12 · The Avon New Cut, south Bristol
photograph Emma Stibbon

The River Avon provides both subject and material for Richard Long. His connection with the immediate environment comes from his earliest memories, as he explains: 'My first natural playground was the cliffs of the Avon Gorge and the towpath by the river. So even as a kid I was fascinated by the enormous tide, and the mud banks, and the wash of the ships as they swept past. You have this wash sweeping up the mud ... muddy creeks ... I guess it's right to say that I have used that experience in my art ... like water, the tides, the mud. All that cosmic energy is there in my work.'[1]

In his monumental mudwork *Muddy Gravity* (p. 101), Richard Long combines the simplicity and directness of an idea with the material substance of the subject. As the watery mud collected from the banks of the River Avon is smeared onto the black gallery wall, the splashes and rhythmic patterns emphasise the energy of his hand and connect us back to the pull of the river. Since the mid-1960s Richard Long has made walking the medium for his art. He records these walks using a pared-down language that references nature and the elements experienced along the way. Two Textworks accompany this mudwork: *A Straight Northward Walk Across Dartmoor 1979* (p. 100) and *Cuckoo Walk an 18 day road walk of 534 miles in Portugal and Spain in the spring of 2014*. These works locate us in time and place, embodying the weather, seasons and the very terrain of the earth.

Our visceral association with the materiality of earth has long been an inspiration for artists. An earlier Bristol artist, Samuel Jackson, also found an earthy connection with the tidal and geological forces of the Avon Gorge. Often drawing and painting directly from nature, in his large watercolour *The Avon Gorge at Sunset* of c.1825 (p. 39) the shadows of the gorge envelop the viewer, with the evening light adding drama as it just catches the top of the limestone cliff walls. His close attention to the mudbanks of the Avon at low tide, and the limestone strata and rock forms of the cliff walls, shows his interest in the new geological surveys being made of the Avon Gorge at the time. His painting both lovingly describes the topography and is a poetic study of light and classical landscape.[2]

The muddy River Avon is also a rich source of inspiration for Andrew Hardwick. Growing up on the family farm that was divided by the M5 motorway and then again by Royal Portbury Dock, his studio is situated on the edge of the Severn Estuary. His tactile paintings draw us in through their material surface, the paint built up with earth materials, plastic and other flotsam gathered from his walks along the banks of the Severn. The painting *Avonmouth, Saltings and Brown Estuary* (p. 89) evokes the muddy tidal space between land and estuary, a liminal borderland of in-between-ness. When I visited Andrew's studio we walked out onto the banks of the Severn behind his studio, situated on an industrial hinterland between Avonmouth Docks and Portishead. On our return, Andrew had to remind engineers that were erecting a new pylon in the adjacent field to open the gate so the cows could reach their water trough. His works remind us that our impact on the Earth is ever encroaching.

Memories of natural environments, and our interference with them, are themes that have recurred throughout Anthony Whishaw's long artistic career, permeated by a lifelong fascination with nature. Moments of assault on nature are keenly felt; for example *Downstream Flow II* of 1996–8 (fig. 13) is a response to his shock at the amount of litter seen on a canal trip through Little Venice around 15 years earlier. *Downstream Flow II* takes an aerial view in his reimagining of the water, incorporating found cups and other flotsam into the paint surface. The sculptural surface of the painting

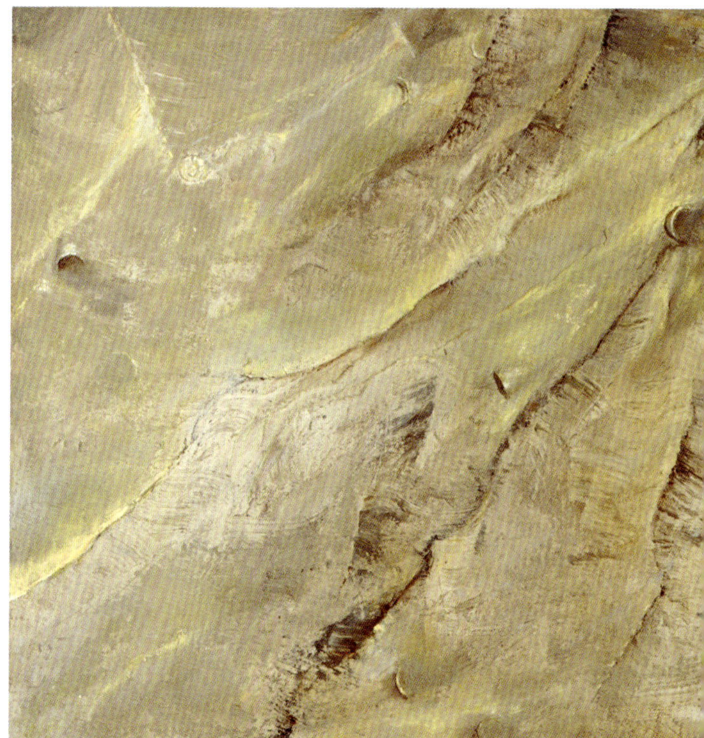

FIG. 13 · **Anthony Whishaw RA RWA** · **b.1930** · ***Downstream Flow II***
1996–8 · mixed media on canvas · 153 x 153 cm
courtesy and © the artist

draws us into the ebb and flow of the water, the floating detritus reminding us that this is a polluted city waterway.

In her work *Shoreline* (p. 85) Susan Derges connects us to the gravitational pull of the Moon on the Earth and its influence on the tidal rise and fall in sea levels. In the 1990s Derges made many photographic prints along the Devon coast at night, using the landscape as her darkroom, where she captured the rolling waves breaking onto her light-sensitive paper. More recently she has revisited this imagery, making a series of polymer photogravure prints through which the preciousness and precariousness of the land and ocean are emphasised by her use of a gold ground overprinted in a deep reddish brown. The resulting images have captured the delicate patterns of a breaking wave on the sandy shoreline. These arrested images of an ever-shifting sea evoke a sense both of time passing and continuity. We are reminded of the cosmic magnitude of the Moon's gravitational pull on the Earth and its impact on the resulting waves that move through the oceans.

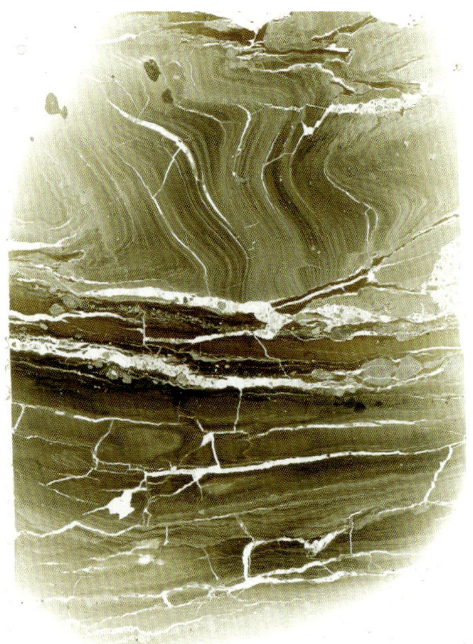

FIG. 14 · **microscope slide showing iceberg-scoured clays and silts retrieved from former Glacial Lake Agassiz, Manitoba, Canada** · 5.3 cm wide
Dr Lorna Linch, School of Applied Sciences, University of Brighton

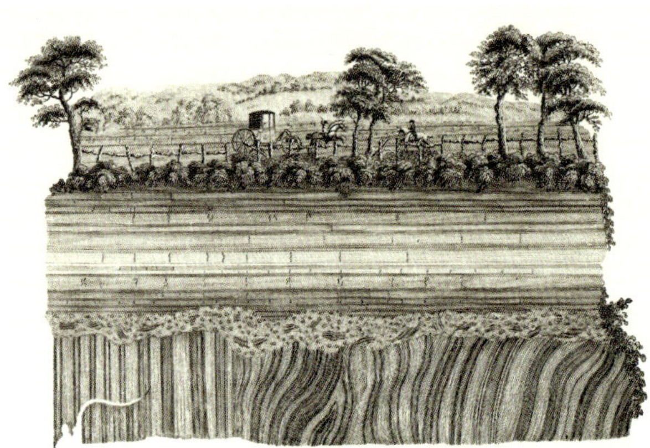

FIG. 15 · **after John Clerk of Eldin FRSE FSAScot** · **1728-1812**
Unconformity at Jedburgh, Borders
1795 · engraving
from James Hutton, *Theory of the Earth* (Edinburgh: Creech, 1795), vol. I, plate III

The formation of the Earth and the natural forces that thrust it into mountains or erode and wash it away as sediments is now understood through the science of geology. In the 1780s and 1790s James Hutton published various stages of his famed *Theory of the Earth*, which established the study of the Earth as a proper science. He was able to show that soils are formed by the weathering of rocks and how layers of sediments accumulate on the Earth's surface. Hutton's work included an engraving based on a drawing by John Clerk of Eldin, a visionary illustration (fig. 15) in which Clerk reveals the world through stratified sections: a series of underlying rocks, sediments and minerals that support the visible flora and fauna that make up our familiar Earth's surface.

The Earth's geological materials can also be observed and analysed on a micro scale. In the research of Dr Lorna Linch, an earth scientist at the University of Brighton, we see a thin-section microscope slide (fig. 14) of iceberg-scoured clays and silts retrieved from the former Glacial Lake Agassiz (Manitoba, Canada). The upper clay and silt layers have been deformed and realigned in response to the stresses imposed by the scraping and scouring of an iceberg moving forwards through the sediments on the lakebed. Detailed observations such as these reveal the history of the Earth by reconstructing past glacial events and the dynamics of former ice sheets.

Our geological understanding of the Earth was profoundly deepened when, in 1815, William Smith made his large map *A Delineation of the Strata of England and Wales, with part of Scotland...* (fig. 16). Smith's observations of geological strata laid the foundations of our grasp of geological time. Contemporary artist Rodney Harris reinvents William Smith's map by embarking on a geological tour of Britain to make his 15-part print based on the original (p. 91). Gathering rock samples from each geological region Harris then ground them into pigments, mixing them with linseed oil. Cutting a jigsaw puzzle of lino relief blocks of each geological area, he printed them in their corresponding pigments. His monumental print shows the texture and quality of each pigment; the squashings of ink as the block is pulled away gives a tangible sense of earth to the printed surface. Harris's own connection to place is specific: coming from a Somerset farming family, he has a deep connection to the earth that resonates in his reimagining of William Smith's map.

The mapping of the Earth also plays a fundamental role in Kathy Prendergast's practice. Her 2010 work *Chimborazo* shows the high volcano summit of that name in Ecuador (p. 115). Chimborazo's summit forms the highest point on the Earth's surface from the centre of the Earth, being located along the planet's equatorial bulge. Prendergast has meticulously hand-coloured the printed map with inks, filling between contour marks with colours that radiate out from the volcano's crater. Her modifications transform the map into a vibrant reworking that suggests both the instability of a volatile terrain and the geopolitics of a mapped cartographic space. Running through her work is a concern with the function of maps, the boundaries of territory and power and what information is omitted. The laborious technique of hand-colouring maps, work often traditionally carried out by women, subtly draws our attention to the politics of gender.

The representation of the Earth is a loaded subject and often problematic. Another artist concerned with contested territories and political boundaries is Mariele Neudecker. Her mixed-media diptych, *We Saw It Coming All Along* (fig. 17),

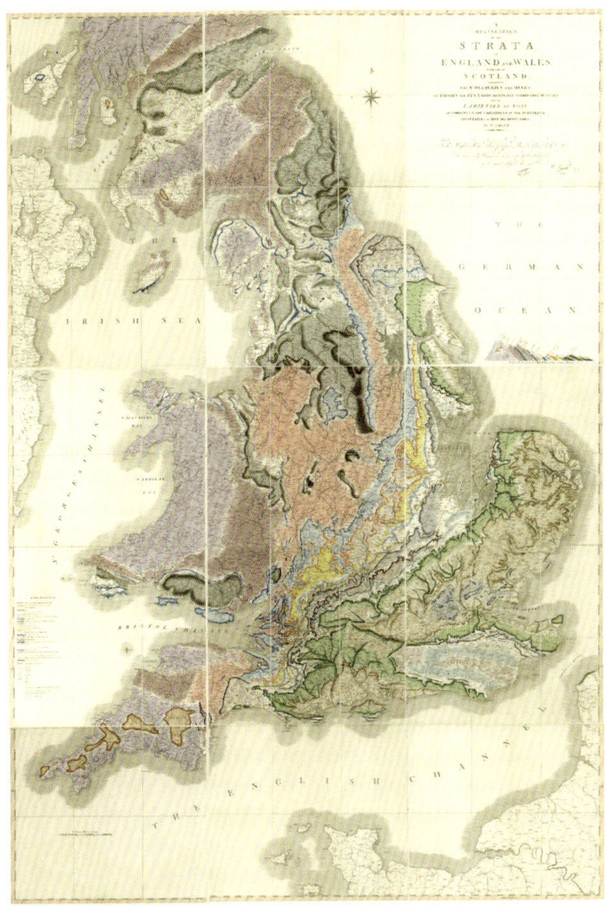

FIG. 16 · **William Smith** · 1769-1839
A Delineation of the Strata of England and Wales, with part of Scotland; exhibiting the collieries and mines, the marshes and fen lands originally overflowed by the sea, and the varieties of soil according to the variations in the substrata, illustrated by the most descriptive names
1815 · hand coloured engraving with watercolour on paper
306 x 186 cm (made up of nine sections)

shows the Russian flag, distorted but just recognisable, the mixed-media glaze poured on like a 'chemical overlay'.[3] The source image is from an online video that went viral at the time (2007), showing Russia claiming Arctic sea-shelf territory by planting their titanium flag on the seabed. Like much of her work, the images are paired, one in landscape

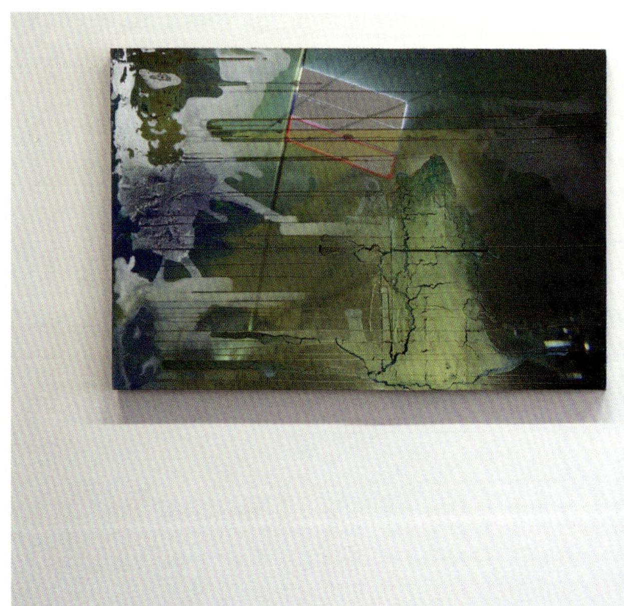
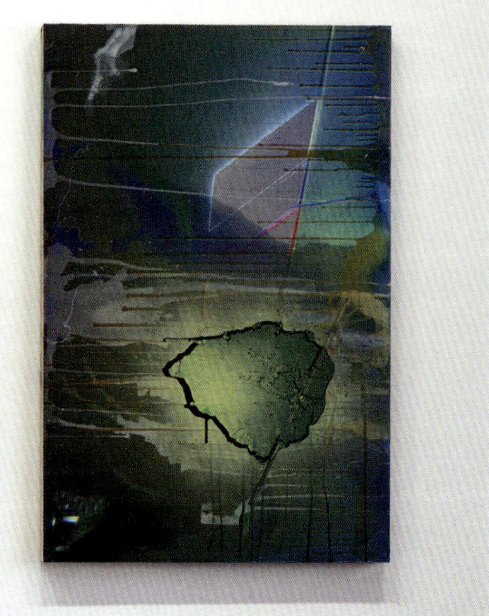

FIG. 17 · **Mariele Neudecker** · **b.1965** · ***We Saw It Coming All Along (1 + 2)***
2019 · diptych · mixed media on archive print on board · 81 x 122 x 5.5 cm and 122 x 81 x 5.5 cm

format the other portrait – a doubling of the image reminiscent of the ever-present eyes of surveillance.

The immensity of geological time is traced through Katie Paterson's *Fossil Necklace* (p. 109), which evidences the history of the Earth through its 170 carved fossil beads. Paterson sourced each fossil to represent life on the planet from the origins of living forms to the present. Working with an expert jeweller, each bead was cut into a sphere and then threaded together. *Fossil Necklace* symbolises the evolution of life on Earth, taking us through the vastness of time. The accompanying key shows the span of geological eras and we are left to consider the brief fraction of time that human presence has been on the Earth.

The out-of-sight ground beneath our feet is often overlooked. In his *Dirt* series (p. 113), Michael Porter makes a forensic study of knotted plant roots and dirt from his garden by carefully laying out the subject alongside his paper. He builds the image using a combination of processes, including photography, digital print and meticulously hand-painted watercolour. Switching between a micro and macro view of the earth, he scrutinises his subject, drawing us into an almost supernatural realism.

Focusing on another seemingly mundane subject, Abigail Lane's *Molehills* (p. 99) represent the physical movement of earth and the interruption of the flat floor space. Often seen as inconvenient, molehills are also funny. As we navigate around them we are reminded of the life that goes on beneath our feet and the transportation of a hidden earth made visible.

An underground world is also explored in Graham Sutherland's drawings *Tin Mine, Various Aspects* (fig. 18) in ink, crayon and wax resist. In 1942 the War Artists' Advisory Committee assigned Sutherland to spend three weeks underground in Cornwall's Geevor tin mine. Sutherland immerses us in this subterranean world through his visceral perspective.

His approach is deeply personal and anthropomorphic, and he renders the mine shafts with an inky blackness that suggests a womblike cavern. Sutherland describes suffering from claustrophobia: 'Once down and walking through the various tunnels – some a mile along – the problem was to avoid getting lost ... Far from the main shaft the sense of remoteness was tangible and the distances seemed endless.'

Climate-related environmental change now signals a critically warming Earth. Rising sea levels and extreme weather events are having a profound impact on the coastal regions and floodplains of our planet. Julian Perry's paintings remind us of the fragility of living life on the edge. *Fanfare 34* (p. 111) depicts the former location of the now abandoned Manor Caravan Park at Happisburgh, north-east Norfolk, before its dramatic retreat due to coastal erosion. The static caravan perches on a sod of earth, floating perilously above the sea, a stark reminder of the instability of the Earth.

Mary Buckland also explored a coastal event – the geological formations caused by a massive landslip affecting the cliffs between Axmouth and Lyme Regis, subsequently published in the engraving *View of the Axmouth Landslip*, 1840 (p. 47). Buckland was a renowned scientific illustrator, and she deftly captured the devastating landslip with her pencil. Like Julian Perry, her observations started out in the field, working on the spot from nature. These images remind us of the vulnerable uncertainty of the very ground we walk on.

Alongside the abundance and fertility of the Earth run our anxieties about the future of the planet and where we are heading. In John Martin's dramatic mezzotint *Bridge over Chaos* (p. 41), we are confronted with the dark abyss, a void of inky blackness. Published in the 1820s to accompany John Milton's epic poem *Paradise Lost*, the plate illustrates the moment Satan, Sin and Death are presented with a passage between Heaven and Hell. The illuminated figures are suspended over a rocky precipice, a vast landscape of the Sublime. The process of mezzotint engraving requires the artist to work from darkness into light, burnishing highlights to illuminate the subject. Martin's visionary image holds us above the chasm, offering a light at the end of the tunnel. Our challenge is how we choose to proceed.

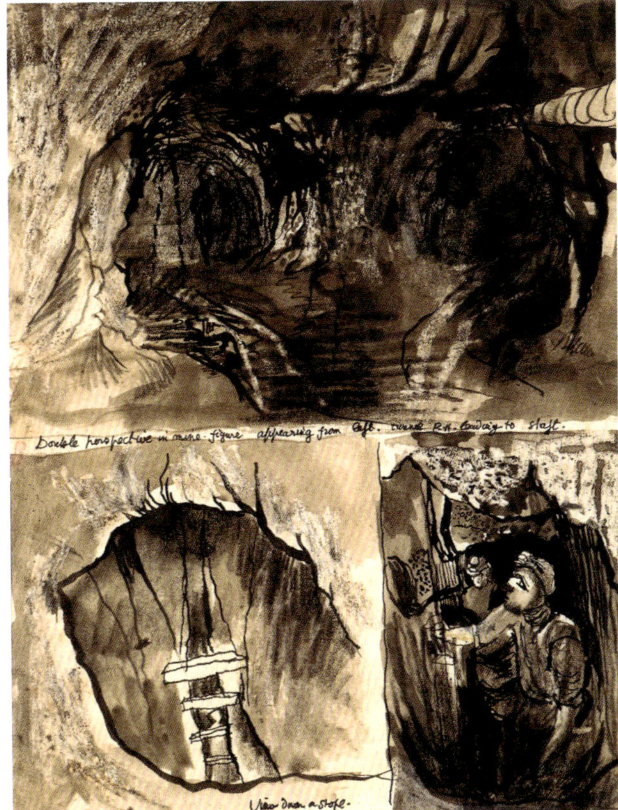

FIG. 18 · **Graham Sutherland OM** · **1903-1980** · ***Tin Mine, Various Aspects***
1942 · pen and ink, crayon and wax resist on paper · 25 x 19 cm
The Ingram Collection of Modern British and Contemporary Art

1. Ben Tufnell (ed.), *Richard Long: Selected Statements & Interviews* (London: Haunch of Venison, 2007).
2. *Absolutely Bizarre! Strange Tales from the Bristol School of Artists (1800–1840)*, exhibition catalogue, Museum of Fine Arts, Bordeaux, 10 June–17 October 2021.
3. Mariele Neudecker in conversation with Emma Stibbon and Nathalie Levi, 20 September 2021.

Catalogue of loan artworks

Christiana Payne

Francis Towne · 1739-1816
The Source of the Arveiron, with Mont Blanc in the Background

1781 · watercolour with pen and ink on four joined sheets of paper · 42.6 x 31.1 cm

Towne was one of the artists who travelled to the Alps in the late eighteenth century in search of the 'sublime' – landscapes which would provoke fear and awe. Vastness, danger, solitude and emptiness all contributed to its effect. The cave of ice below the Glacier des Bois in the Vale of Chamonix, out of which the river Arveyron [sic] flowed, was one of the most famous sights in the region. Visitors compared the frozen shapes formed by the ice to a temple, a palace or a cathedral.[1]

Towne made this drawing on the spot on 17 September 1781, using two openings in his sketchbook to draw the upper and lower parts and afterwards piecing them together. The colours would have been applied in the studio: cold whites and blues for the ice cave and glacier, brown for the rock, bluish greens for the mountains beyond. Finally, he would go over the outlines in pen and ink.

Towne had little success in his lifetime: he had to work as a drawing master to support himself, and it was only in the early twentieth century that he received the recognition he deserved. This drawing was amongst the 17 signed Towne drawings bought by Paul Oppé in 1910 for just 25 shillings (£1.25). In an influential article of 1920, Oppé praised Towne for his mastery of pattern, and he has been a source of inspiration for several abstract artists. Recently, however, Timothy Wilcox has shown how committed he also was to the pursuit of truth.[2]

1. Timothy Wilcox, *Francis Towne* (London: Tate Gallery Publishing, 1997), pp. 101–5.
2. Ibid., pp. 25–6.

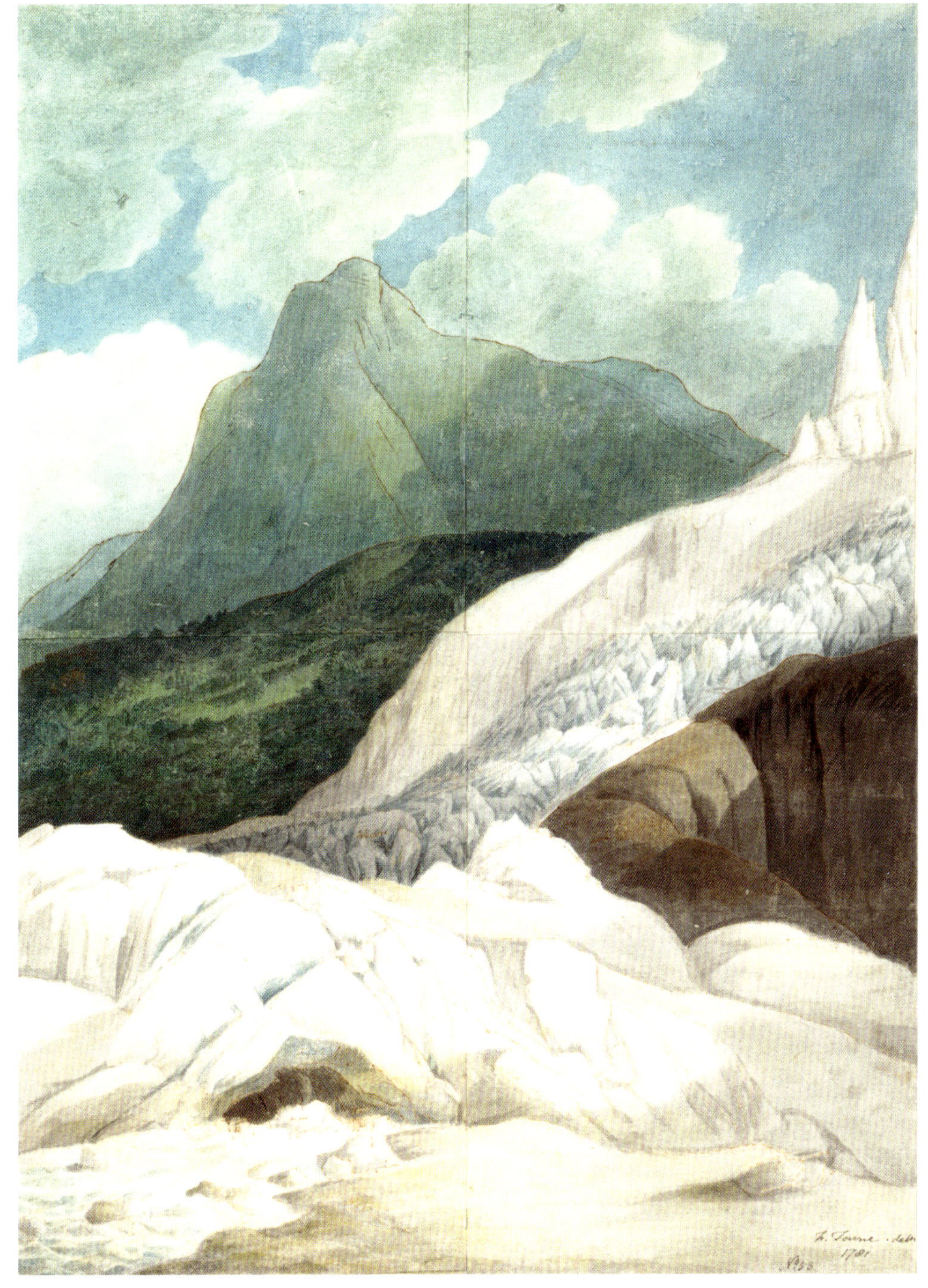
F. Towne . delt
1781

Thomas Gainsborough RA FRSA · 1727-1788
Romantic Landscape with Sheep at a Spring

*c.*1783 · oil on canvas · 153.7 x 186.7 cm

This painting, with its prominent rocks in the foreground and a sunlit mountain in the distance, dates from a time in Gainsborough's life when he was varying his subject matter and aiming for greater grandeur. In around 1782 he made a tour of England's West Country, and in 1783 he wrote to a friend that he was going to visit 'the Lakes in Cumberland & Westmorland'. He went on to say 'I purpose to mount all the Lakes at the next exhibition, in the great stile [sic].'[1] Gainsborough's conception of the 'great stile' included homage to the famous seventeenth-century landscape painters, Claude Lorrain and Gaspard Dughet.

The two huge rocks in the left-hand middle ground may have been suggested by something he had seen in the West Country. They loom rather threateningly over the idyllic pastoral scene, suggesting that he was also gesturing to the current preoccupation with the sublime.

The painting, which is much larger than most of his landscapes, was given by his daughter Margaret to the Royal Academy in 1799, after his death. She presented it 'in compliance with the intention of her late father'. Rather than being a diploma work (which he was not required to supply), it has been suggested that it was originally meant as the painting for the Royal Academy Council Chamber that Gainsborough had promised in 1787.[2] He had withdrawn his paintings from the annual exhibition in 1784, thereafter exhibiting only in his own house, and he perhaps meant to make amends for the quarrel.

1. John Hayes, *The Landscape Paintings of Thomas Gainsborough: A Critical Text and Catalogue Raisonné* (London: Philip Wilson Publishers, 1982), vol. I, p. 161.
2. Ibid., vol. II, p. 505.

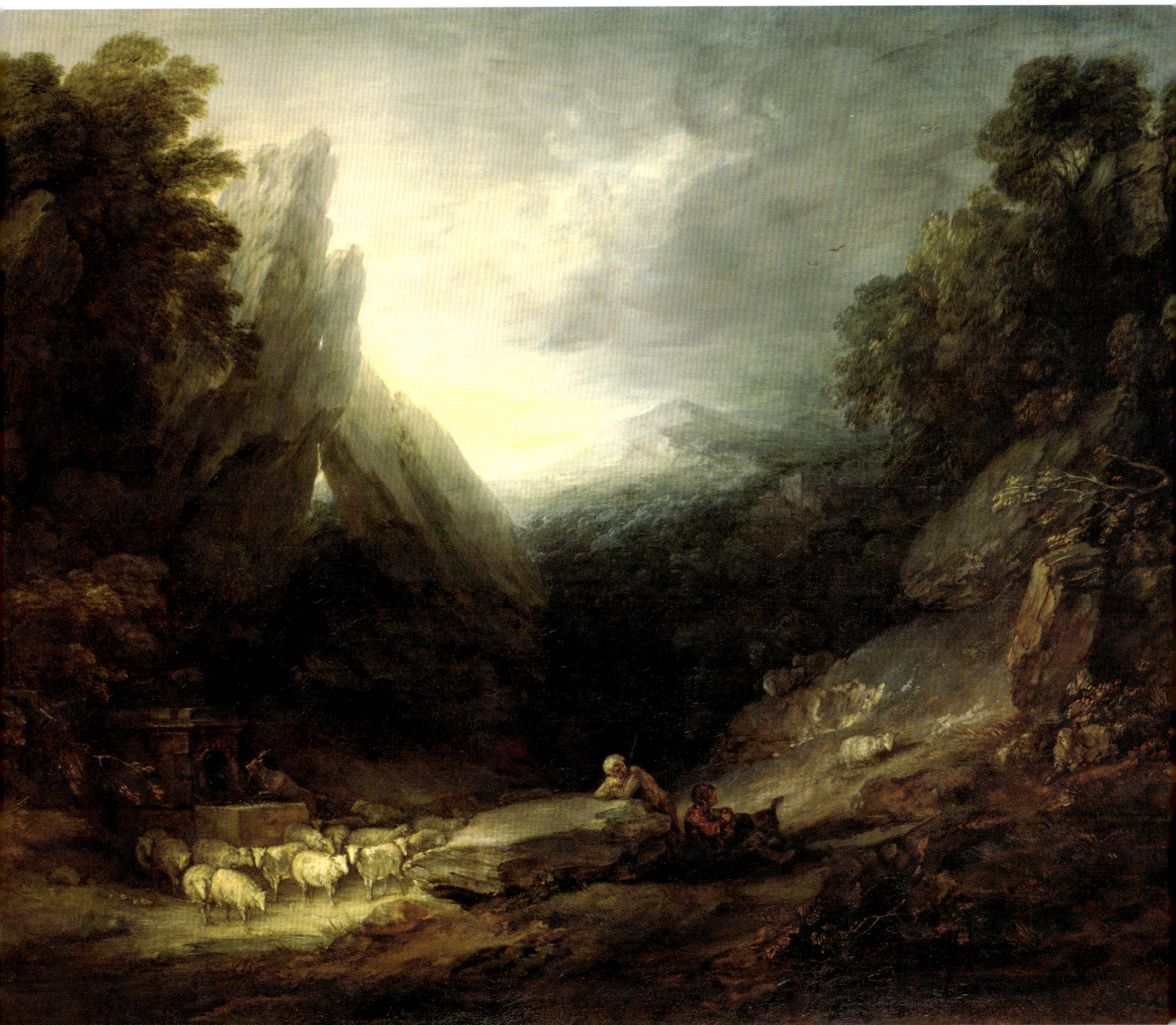

Philip James de Loutherbourg RA · 1740-1812
An Avalanche in the Alps

1803 · oil on canvas · 109.9 x 160 cm
Tate: presented by the Friends of the Tate Gallery, 1965 • photo: Tate

This painting was originally exhibited at the Royal Academy in 1804, with a topographically exact title: 'An avalanche or ice fall, on the Alps near the Scheideck, in the valley of Lauterbrunnen'. De Loutherbourg had visited this area in 1787, although there is no evidence that he actually witnessed an avalanche.[1]

The idea behind the 'sublime' was that situations that would in reality be extremely frightening, painful and distressing could excite pleasurable emotions when represented in art and literature. Here de Loutherbourg shows us several stages in the distancing effect. The human beings in the chalet, swept down the mountainside by the avalanche, are already doomed. The man, woman and dogs on the path are too busy praying or running away to feel a sense of the sublime. The traveller on the extreme left, however, is at a safe enough distance to enjoy the spectacle, and his stance suggests how the viewer of the painting should react to it. From the comfort of a drawing room or gallery, we are meant to feel a thrill of 'delicious horror'.

De Loutherbourg had a successful career as a designer of theatre sets, as well as being a landscape painter. In 1781 he created the 'Eidophusikon', a miniature theatre in which painted landscapes were accompanied by sound and light effects. One can imagine the dramatic contrasts of light and shade, the thunderous rumbles and crashes, that would accompany a scene such as this one.

1. Olivier Lefeuvre, *Philippe-Jacques de Loutherbourg* (Paris: Arthena, 2012), p. 311.

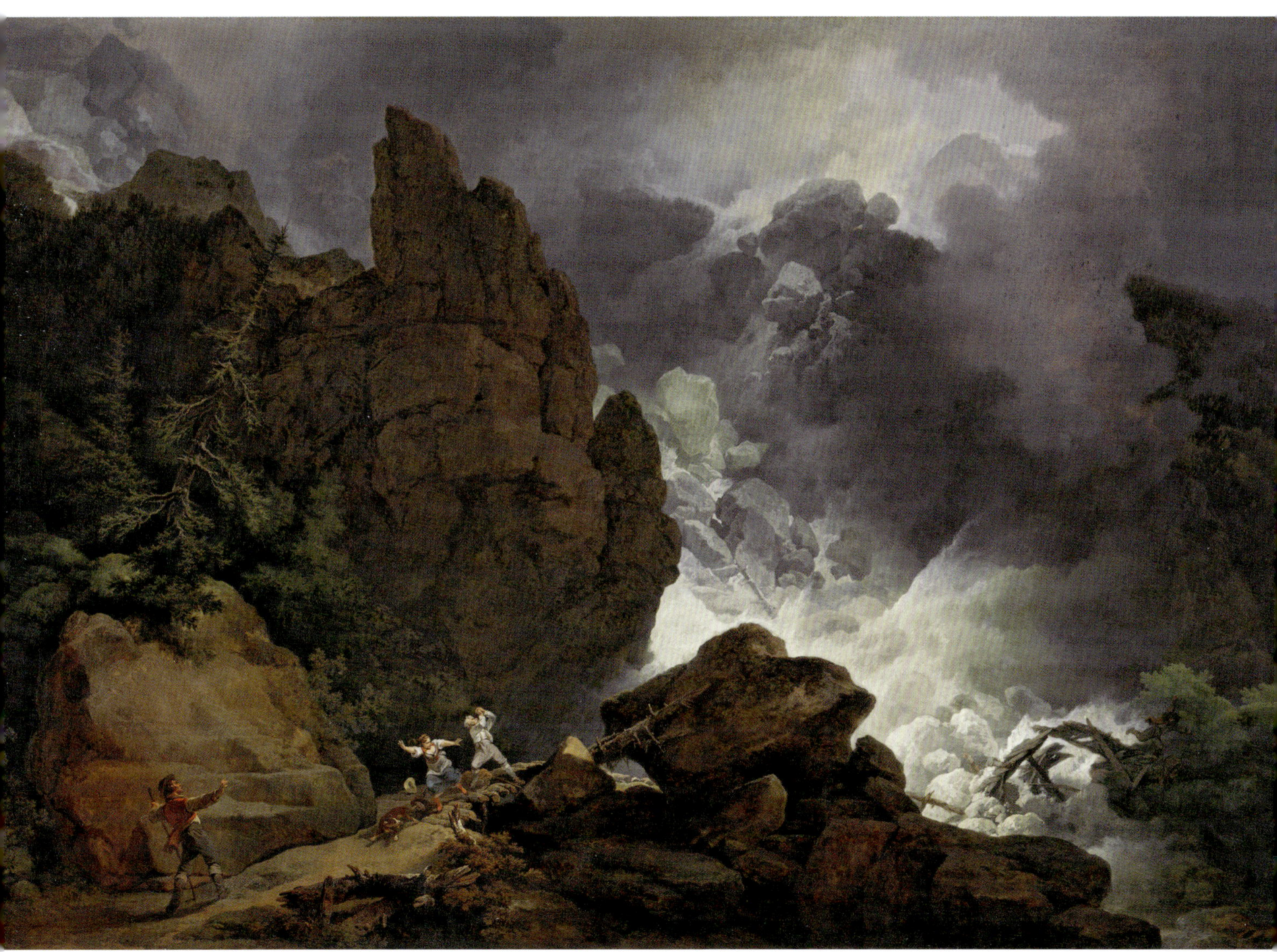

J.M.W. Turner RA · 1775-1851
Cassiobury Park: Reaping

*c.*1809 · oil on oak panel · 90.2 x 121.9 cm
Tate: accepted by the nation as part of the Turner Bequest, 1956 • photo: Tate

At a time when bread was the staple item in the diet, representations of the wheat harvest were a popular way of celebrating the productiveness of the earth. This may seem an unusual subject for Turner, but it dates from a time in his life when he was taking a great interest in agriculture. Britain was at war with Napoleonic France, and the home production of food was made more important still by the French blockade of the English ports, a situation which Turner explicitly addressed in his poetry.

The technique of the painting is similar to that of his large open-air studies in oil, but it is painted on an oak panel, which would have been difficult to manoeuvre in the field, so it may have been done in the studio. Nevertheless, it gives a vivid impression of the heat of a summer's day: some of the reapers, and a dog, have fallen into an exhausted sleep, and the women have stripped to their bodices.

The painting was probably intended for George Capel-Coningsby (1757–1839), the 5th Earl of Essex and owner of Cassiobury Park. Turner stayed there in August 1809 and made studies of reaping and a harvest home in his sketchbooks. He also began a large painting of the harvest home (Tate), but neither this nor *Cassiobury Park: Reaping* was finished, perhaps because Turner felt uncomfortable including so many figures on such a large scale. His interest in harvest scenes continued to be explored in his watercolours, however.

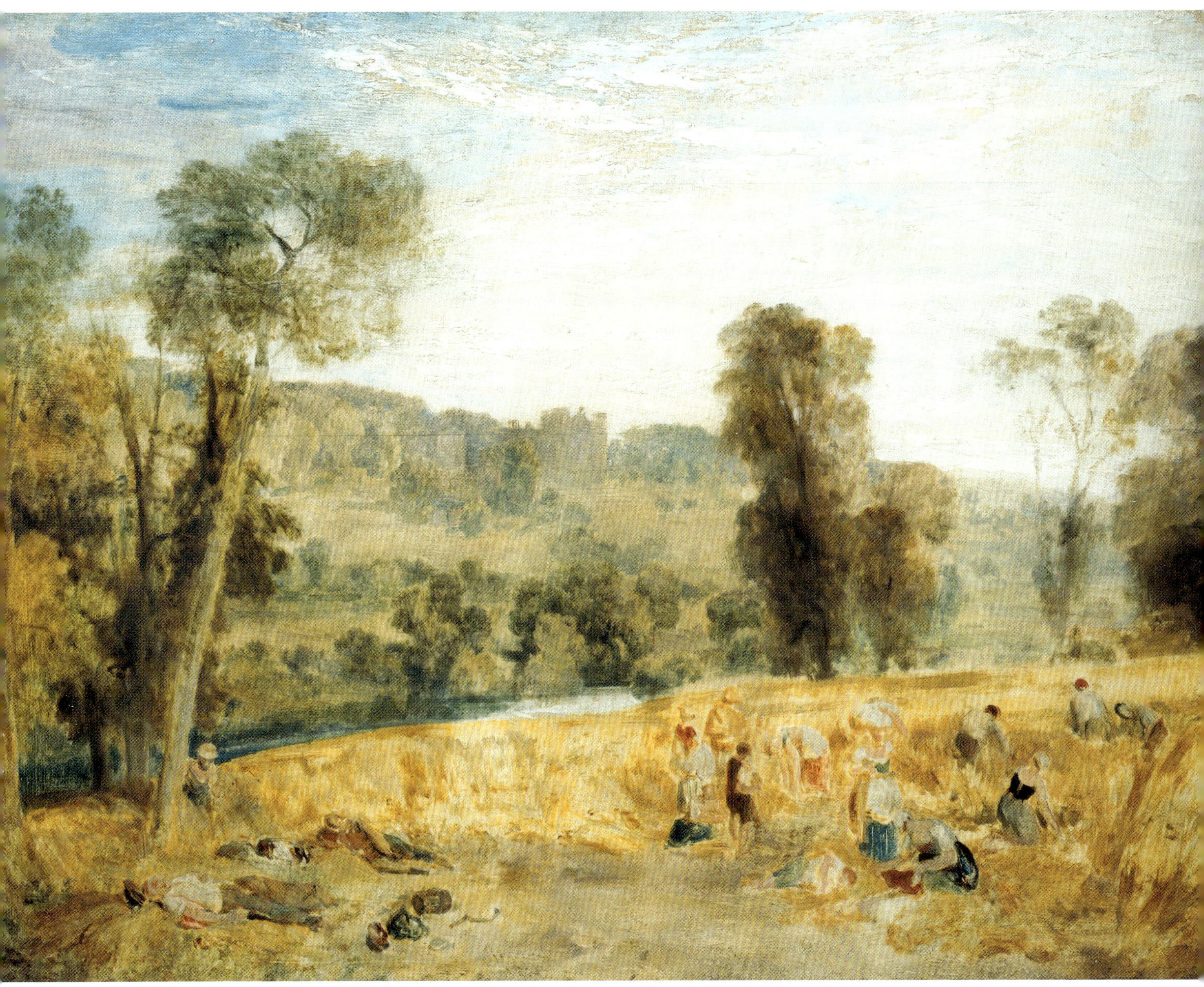

John Constable RA · 1776-1837
Golding Constable's Kitchen Garden

1815 · oil on canvas · 33 x 50.8 cm
Colchester and Ipswich Museums Service: Ipswich Borough Council Collection

This painting was executed in the summer of 1815, the year the Battle of Waterloo brought the Napoleonic Wars to an end. Several artists painted or exhibited harvest scenes in this year, seeing them as patriotic celebrations of the fertility of British soil. The picture was painted from nature, but not in the field: Constable worked in an upper room in his father's house, combining the conveniences of the studio with the advantages of having his subject directly in front of him.

Using meticulous brushwork on a small scale, Constable shows us the whole economy of a village. Ripe wheatfields and meadows, vegetable gardens, a windmill for grinding corn, farmhouses, cottages and sheds are laid out as if on a map. In the far distance on the left, reaping is taking place, and we can just make out a loaded waggon and the white shirts of the harvesters. Not only the garden in the foreground, but also the wheatfields, meadows and windmill belonged to Constable's father, so that he is, in a sense, declaring his own possession of the land. Like its companion, *Golding Constable's Flower Garden* (1815, Ipswich Borough Council), the painting was never exhibited or sold in Constable's lifetime. It seems that the two works were exercises in painting entire pictures directly from nature.

The painting had strong personal resonance for Constable. In addition to his father's land, the view includes, just to the right of centre, the Rectory. This was the home of Dr Rhudde, who represented at that time a powerful obstacle to Constable's marriage to Maria Bicknell.

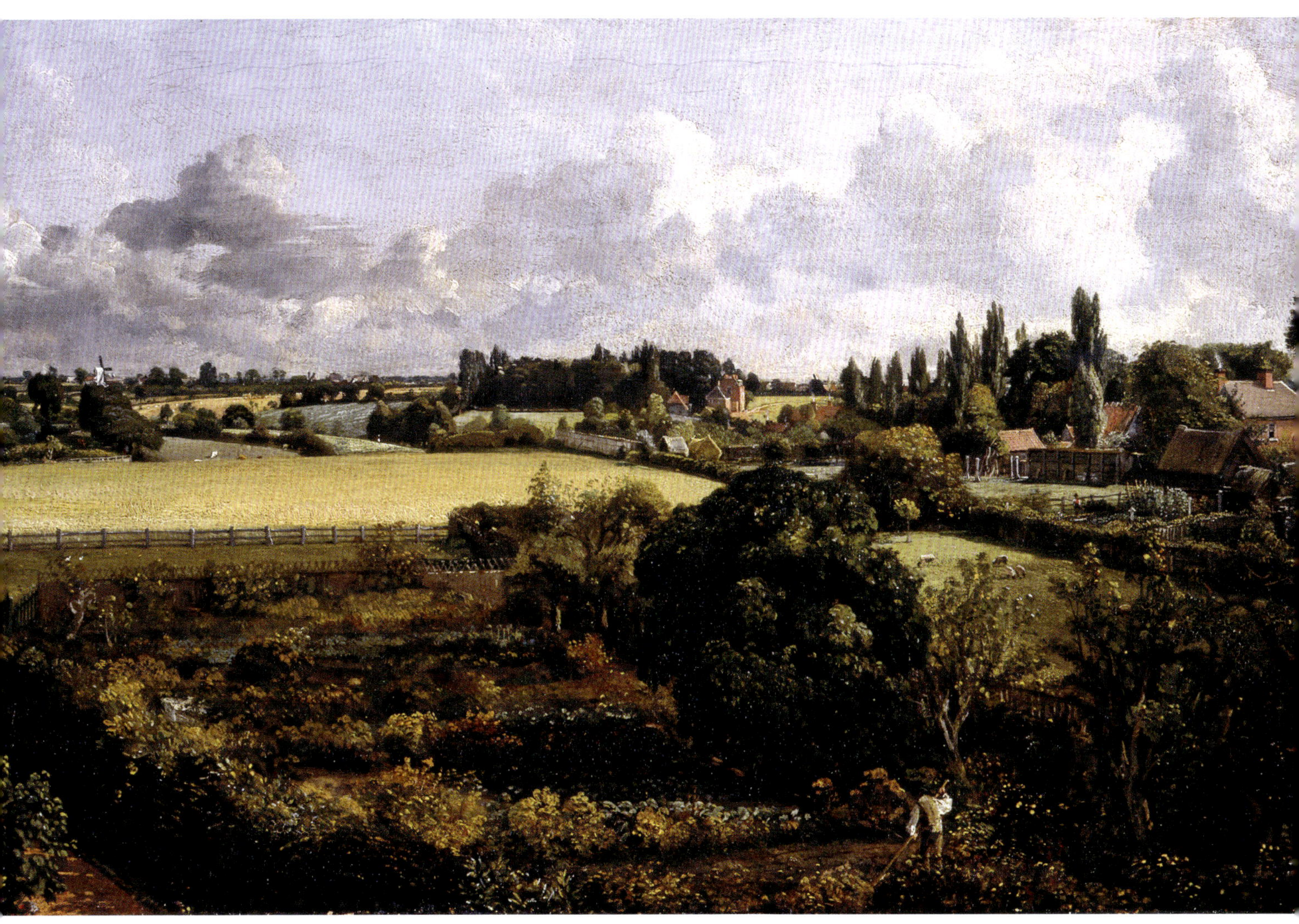

William Blake · 1757-1827
Thenot and Colinet Converse and Sabrina's Silvery Flood

illustrations for *The Pastorals of Virgil* by Robert John Thornton · 1821
wood engravings · 3.3 x 7.5 cm and 3.3 x 7.3 cm

Towards the end of his life, Blake was commissioned to produce 17 designs for a schoolbook, *The Pastorals of Virgil*, published by Dr Robert Thornton. Blake's designs illustrate a poem by Ambrose Philips (bap. 1674–1749) written in imitation of Virgil, describing a conversation between two shepherds, Thenot and Colinet.

Blake had never made wood engravings before, and he cut his blocks directly, so that the lines of the engraved block appear white, rather than following the usual practice of imitating the black lines of a drawing. His style is deliberately primitive, suggesting the delights of the simple life, lived in harmony with nature. Thornton was worried about the unusual characteristics of Blake's illustrations, and included a disclaimer in the book to the effect that they 'display less art than genius, and are much admired by some eminent painters'.

These tiny prints had a huge influence on two of Blake's young admirers, Samuel Palmer and Edward Calvert. Palmer described them as 'visions of little dells, and nooks, and corners of Paradise ... There is in all such a mystic and dreamy glimmer as penetrates and kindles the inmost soul, and gives complete and unreserved delight, unlike the gaudy daylight of this world.'[1] Calvert followed Blake in taking up wood engraving, and adopting some of his subject matter, but developed the technique in a much more sophisticated way.

1. A.H. Palmer, *Life and Letters of Samuel Palmer* (London: Seely & Co., 1892), pp. 15–16.

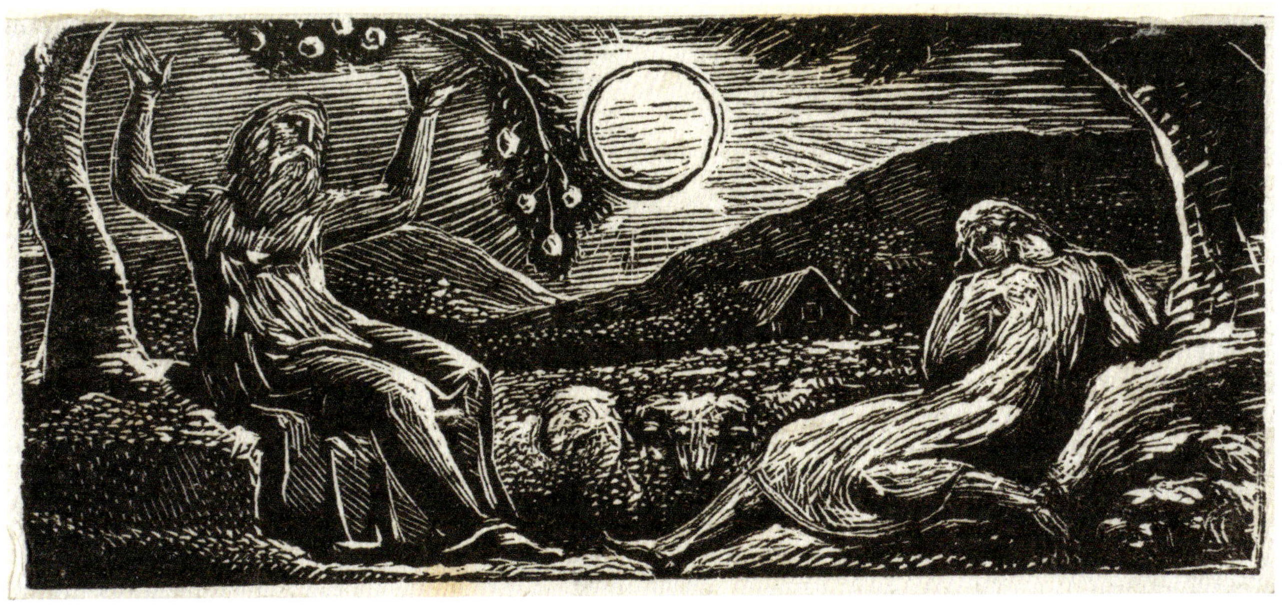

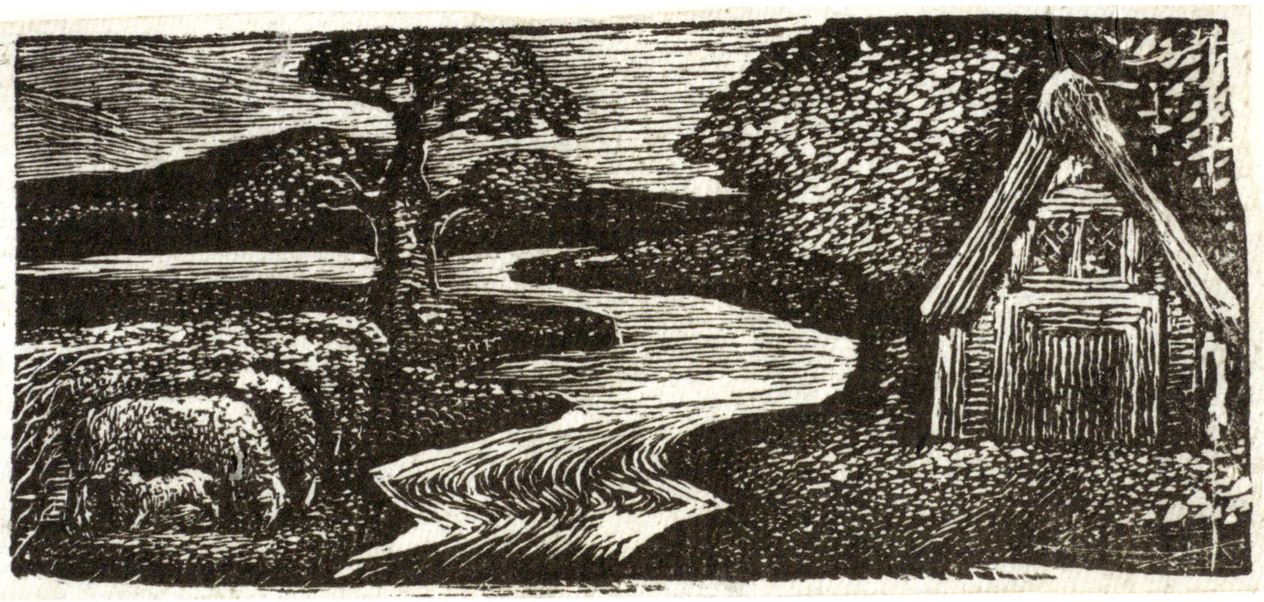

John Sell Cotman · 1782-1842
View of Domfront, from the Rock of Tertre Grisière

1823 · pencil and watercolour on paper · 29.5 x 41.6 cm
The Courtauld, London (Samuel Courtauld Trust) · photograph © The Courtauld

Cotman visited the medieval town of Domfront, in southern Normandy, in August 1820 when he was collecting material for his *Architectural Antiquities of Normandy* (1822). While staying there he experienced grand storms with tremendous rain and thunder, and had to take advantage of short intervals between showers to make his drawings. As he wrote in a letter, 'the clearing up of the mist, & passing clouds over the forest gave inexpressible beauty to an already most superb & fine situation'.[1] In his rendering of the scene, he over-dramatises the situation of the town and exaggerates the tilt of the rocks, reflecting the contemporary idea of the sublime.

However, the watercolour also looks forward to a more scientific and geological approach to the study of the basic materials of the Earth. Cotman was clearly fascinated by the configuration of the rocks (sandstone metamorphosed into a hard quartzite) on which the town was built. Cotman's patron, Dawson Turner, had an interest in geology, and knew Charles Lyell, later to become famous as the author of *Principles of Geology* (1830-33). Lyell was a visitor to Dawson Turner's house in 1817, when Cotman might have participated in discussions on the topic.[2] At this stage in his life Lyell was still a student at Oxford, attending lectures by geologist William Buckland. Lyell's interpretation of geological processes as the steady accumulation of minute changes over enormously long spans of time was a major influence on the thinking of Charles Darwin as he developed his theory of evolution.

1. David Hill, 'The Tertre Grisière at Domfront ...', https://cotmania.org/works-of-art/42736, accessed 24 November 2021.
2. Timothy Wilcox, *Cotman in Normandy* (London: Dulwich Picture Gallery, 2012), p. 82.

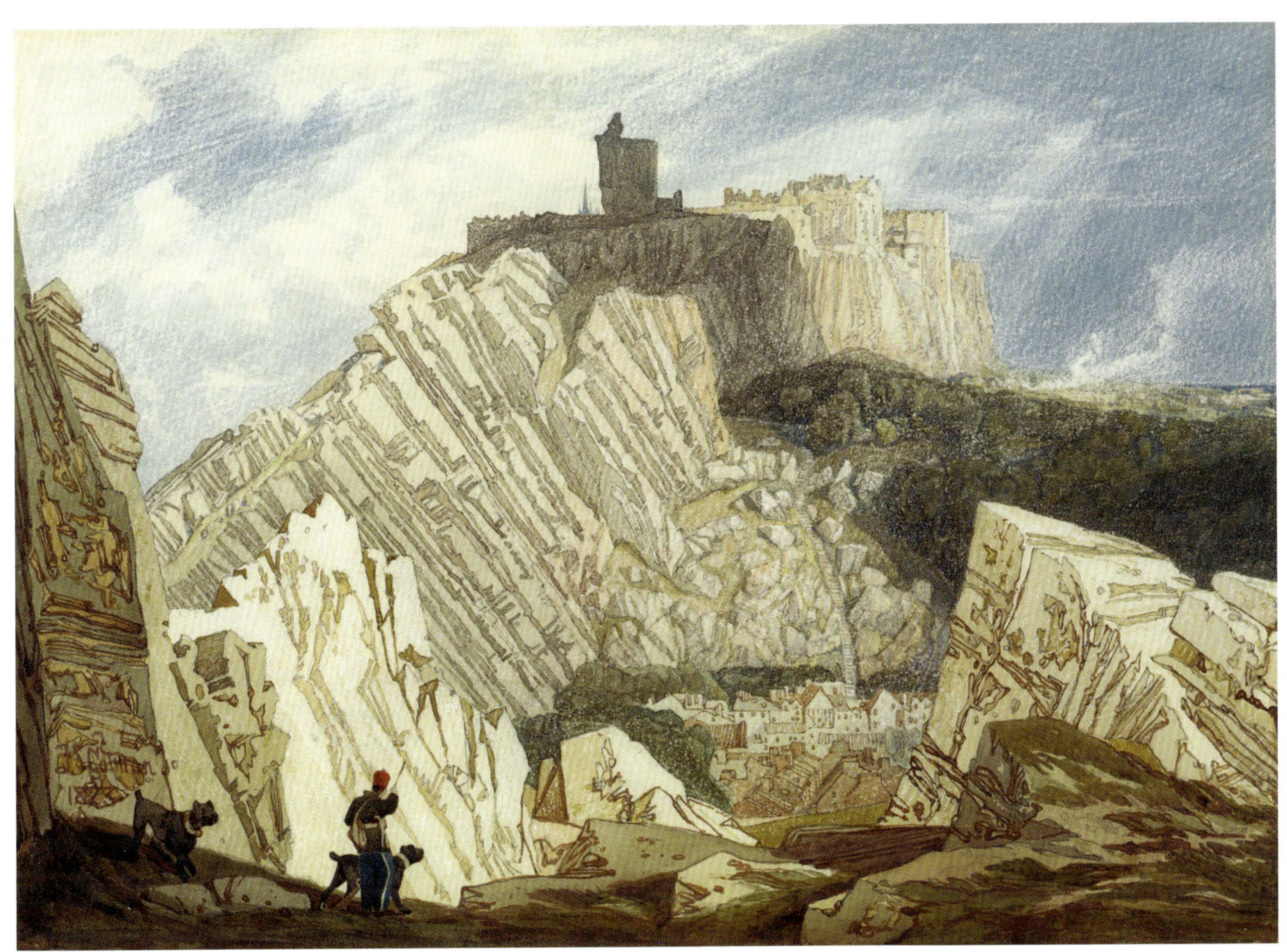

Samuel Jackson · **1794-1869**
The Avon Gorge at Sunset

*c.*1825 · watercolour on paper · 29.7 x 44.8 cm
purchased with the assistance of the Victoria and Albert Museum Purchase Grant Fund and the Friends of Bristol Art Gallery, 1982 • Bristol Culture: Bristol Museum and Art Gallery

The dramatic scenery of the Avon Gorge has been a source of inspiration to artists in Bristol for centuries. North of where the Clifton Suspension Bridge now spans the gorge, the River Severn winds through rugged limestone cliffs on its way to the Severn Estuary and the Bristol Channel. Jackson, the so-called 'father' of the early nineteenth-century Bristol School of Artists, painted this view several times.

In this watercolour, the river is calm and the landscape looks serene and idyllic. On the far horizon we can see Cook's Folly, a prospect tower that was built in the late seventeenth century and demolished in 1892. The cliffs known as Sea Walls, on the right, have been blasted with gunpowder to quarry stone for the building boom that was going on in the city of Bristol at the time. The warm light of the setting sun gives them a reddish glow and draws attention to the way they have been exposed, with the grassy slopes of Clifton Down above them threatened by overhang and erosion. Below the cliffs are four flat-bottomed boats, used to transport the stone and specially developed for the mudbanks that are a feature of the river at low tide.

Jackson was born in Bristol and spent his life in the city. He was one of the organisers of the first exhibition by local artists at the new Bristol Institution in 1824, and in 1832 he was the most eminent participant in the first exhibition of the Bristol Society of Artists.

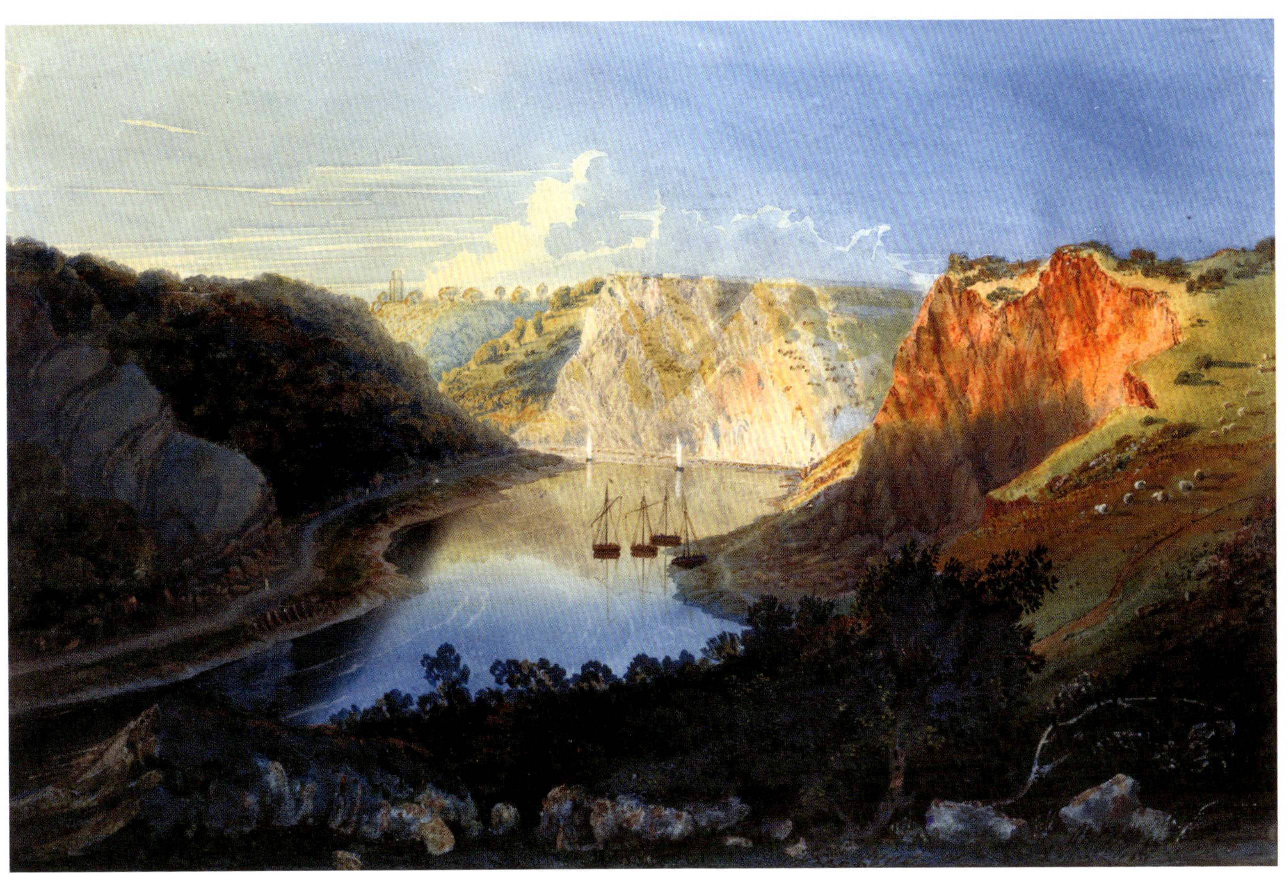

John Martin · 1789-1854
Bridge over Chaos

1824-5 · mezzotint · 25.4 x 35.6 cm
plate from *The Paradise Lost of John Milton, with illustrations designed and engraved by John Martin (1789-1854)*, in two volumes (London: Septimus Prowett, 1827)

In 1824 Samuel Prowett, an American publisher, commissioned Martin to produce a series of illustrations to John Milton's *Paradise Lost* (1667). Martin was already famous for his 'sublime' landscapes of biblical scenes, and his Milton illustrations were readily received as works of genius. Unusually, the artist created his designs on the plates as he worked, rather than working from an existing drawing. The design of *Bridge over Chaos* is regarded as 'the artist's supreme visionary conception of the underworld ... the most sought after of all Martin's printed works'.[1]

This print illustrates the passage in the poem (Book X, ll. 312-47) after the expulsion of Adam and Eve from the Garden of Eden, when Satan admires the stupendous bridge that has been built by Sin (his fair daughter) and Death (his not so fair grandson) over Chaos, connecting this world with Hell. The bridge over the abyss enables Sin and Death to travel easily between Hell, where Satan reigns, and the world, where they can cause endless trouble for humankind.

Martin made use of the wide tonal range that was possible in mezzotint, from the deep blacks of the depths of Chaos to the brilliant white of the figure of Satan (also known as Lucifer, 'bringer of light'). The huge scale of the bridge over Chaos echoes such artistic precedents as Roman aqueducts, but also parallels contemporary plans for engineering projects, such as the Thames Tunnel, which was begun in 1825.

1. Michael J. Campbell, *John Martin: Visionary Printmaker* (Campbell Fine Art/York City Art Gallery, 1992), p. 61.

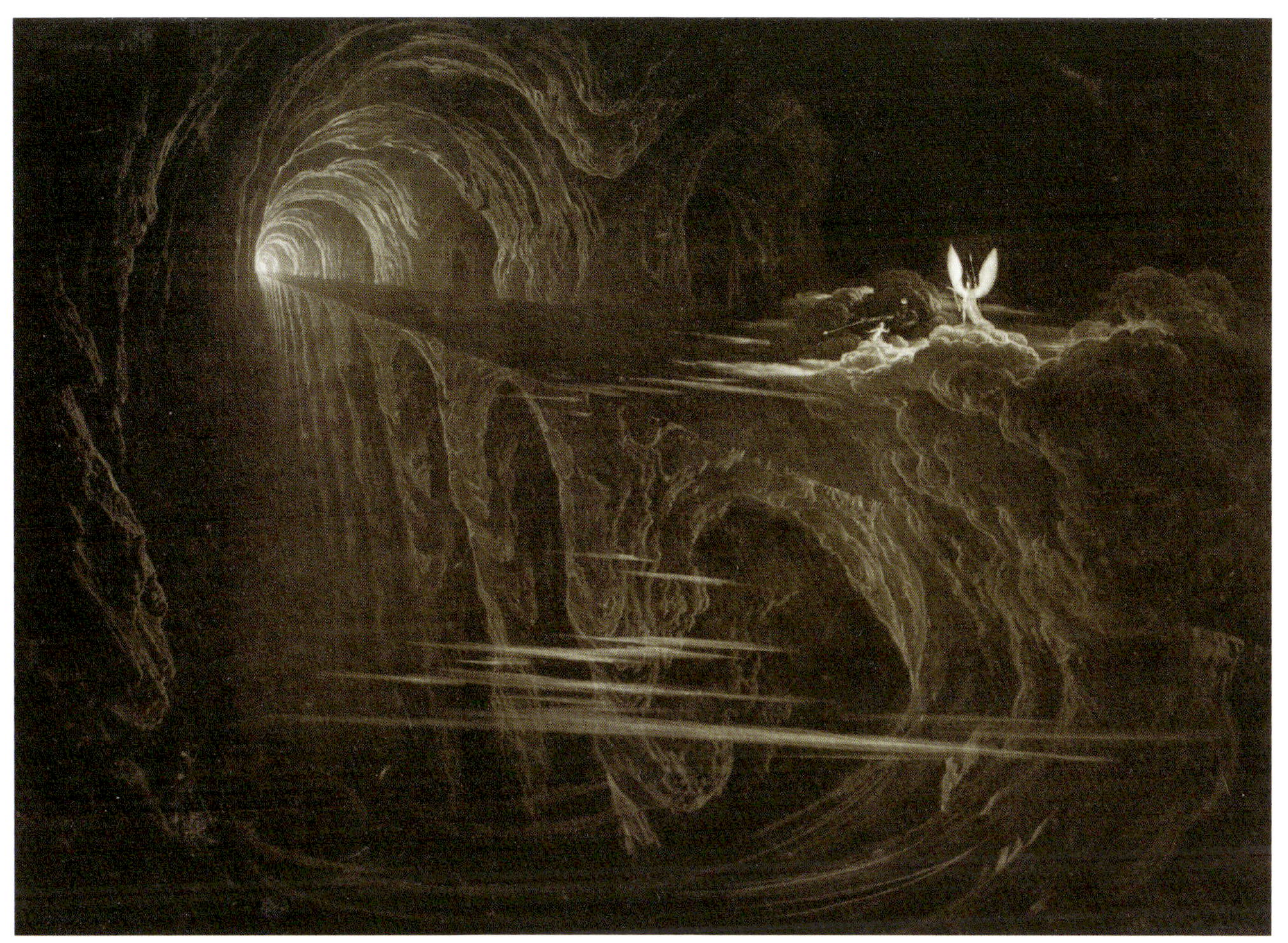

William Henry Hunt · 1790-1864
The Head Gardener

*c.*1825 · pen and brown ink, ink wash, watercolour and bodycolour over graphite on paper · 28.8 x 34.7 cm

The Courtauld, London (Samuel Courtauld Trust) · photograph © The Courtauld

This is thought to be a portrait of James Anderson (1797–1842), head gardener for the 5th Earl of Essex. Anderson collected plants in Africa and South America, and later became Superintendent of the Botanic Gardens in Sydney, Australia. During his lifetime, the range of fruits, vegetables and flowers from other countries that could be grown under glass in Britain was expanding rapidly. The display of produce shown here is a testament to the good management of the Cassiobury Park estate and the wealth of its owner, who was also a patron of J.M.W. Turner (p. 30).

The watercolour was probably exhibited at the Old Water-Colour Society, in London, in 1825, along with portraits of a poacher and a gamekeeper. Hunt painted many small-scale watercolours of estate servants in the 1820s. Some of these were commissioned by their employers, but others were painted for the market. Hunt had a particular interest in gardeners and the exotic fruits they propagated, and he went on to become famous as a still-life painter, his repertoire including grapes with their soft bloom, as well as birds' nests.

As Joanna Selborne has pointed out, this watercolour includes a dazzling array of exotic and highly prized fruits and vegetables: pineapples, melons, grapes, peaches and nectarines, celery, cucumber and artichokes, as well as the more everyday vegetables such as cabbages.[1]

1. Joanna Selborne and Christiana Payne, *William Henry Hunt: Country People* (London: Courtauld Gallery, 2017), pp. 40–43.

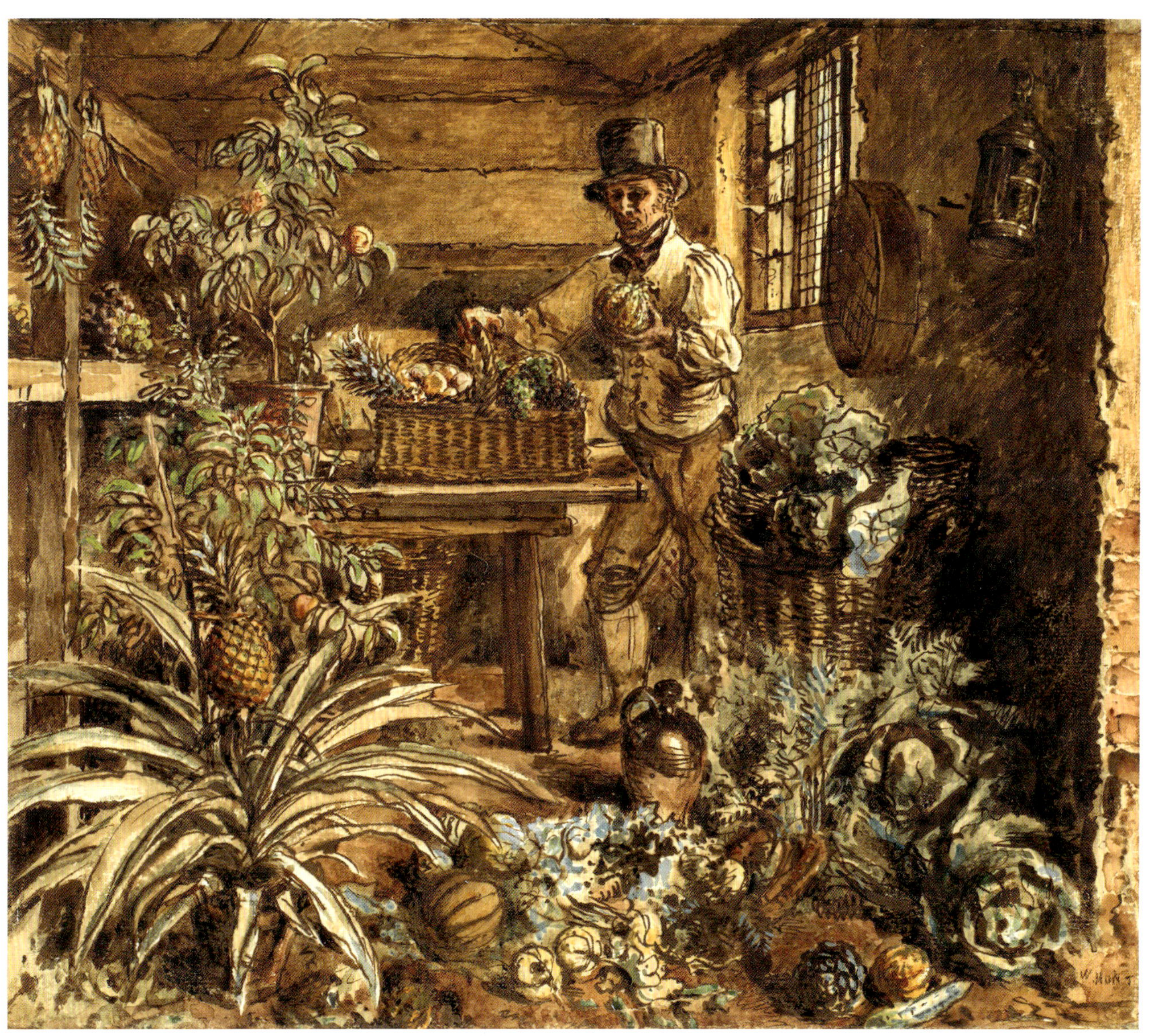
W. HUNT

Edward Calvert · 1799-1883
The Cyder Feast

1828 · wood engraving on paper · 7.6 x 12.7 cm
Tate: presented by S. Calvert 1912 • photo: Tate

In the 1820s, Calvert and his close friend Samuel Palmer produced prints and drawings that celebrated the fecundity of the earth, partly inspired by William Blake's illustrations to Virgil. Palmer took up residence in the village of Shoreham, in Kent, where he and his friends would walk in the moonlight, read poetry, and drink the cider produced by the local farmers. They saw the agricultural activities surrounding them as part of a tradition stretching back to classical times, and particularly appreciated old-fashioned processes such as the use of draught oxen rather than horses.

In this print apples are being crushed in a circular mill powered by oxen, and then the pulp is placed in a press to squeeze out the juice. The emphasis is on the celebration of abundance. Baskets are piled so high with apples that they spill out onto the ground; the juice gushes out of the mill and the press. Blake-like figures dance in front of a huge harvest moon.

Earlier impressions of this print included the lettering 'BY THE GIFT OF GOD IN CHRIST', but Calvert later cut this from the block. He had always been interested in the pagan deities, especially the rustic god Pan, and his later paintings often take their subjects from Greek mythology.

Palmer wrote of this print: 'I don't set up like a judge, but like a blind baby feeling for the breast knows the taste of milk, with a somewhat precocious appetite for cream. I *find* the cream in your *Cider Press*, which, in poetic richness, beats anything I know, ancient or modern.'[1]

1. R. Lister (ed.), *The Letters of Samuel Palmer* (Oxford: Clarendon Press, 1974), vol. I, pp. 52–3.

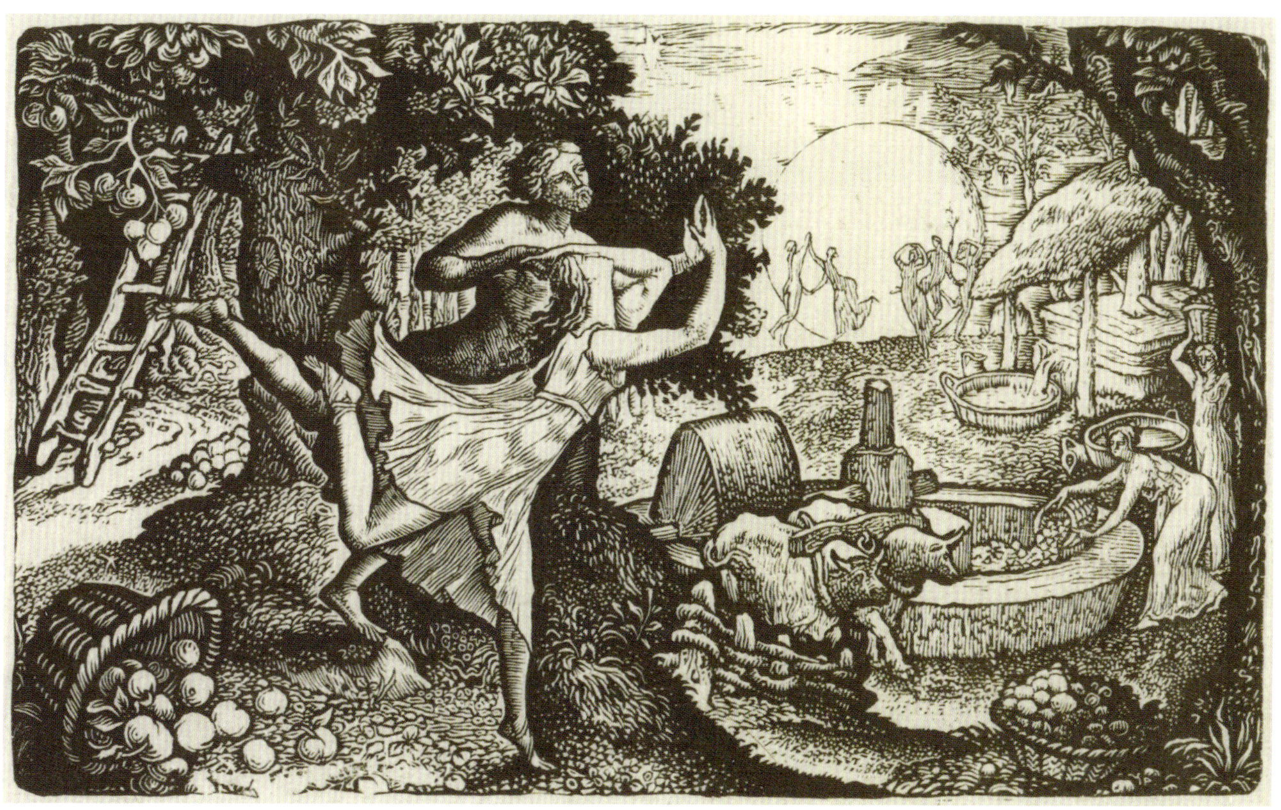

Mary Buckland · 1797-1857
View of the Axmouth Landslip

1839 · watercolour on paper · 56 x 91 cm

At midnight on Christmas Day 1839, the inhabitants of two cottages near Lyme Regis found the floors of their houses rising upwards towards the ceiling. A massive landslip broke off fifty acres from the mainland, leaving a 'tremendous chasm extending three quarters of a mile from east to west and varying in breadth from two hundred to four hundred feet'. This formed the area now known as the Undercliff.[1]

The geologist Dr William Buckland and his wife Mary were staying nearby, and they hastened to the scene, where Mary, a skilled scientific illustrator, made pencil sketches of the chasm. These provided the basis for prints, and also for large drawings, like this one, that could be used by Buckland to illustrate his lectures. Buckland's explanation, that prolonged rain in the autumn had saturated the layer of sand beneath the chalk cliffs, turning it into quicksand, is still favoured today.

In the summer of 1840 fifteen of the fifty acres in the chasm (which had dropped fifty feet from their previous level) produced a fine crop of wheat and turnips. Visitors flocked to see this 'miraculous' harvest.

Mary Buckland began her career as a teenager, producing illustrations and providing specimens for George Cuvier, the famous palaeontologist. She made models of fossils, repaired broken fossils, and helped her husband by providing illustrations for his books, as well as taking dictation, editing and even writing parts of his texts herself. She also gave birth to, and partially educated, nine children.

1. E.O. Gordon, *The Life and Correspondence of William Buckland* (London: J. Murray, 1894), pp. 173-5.

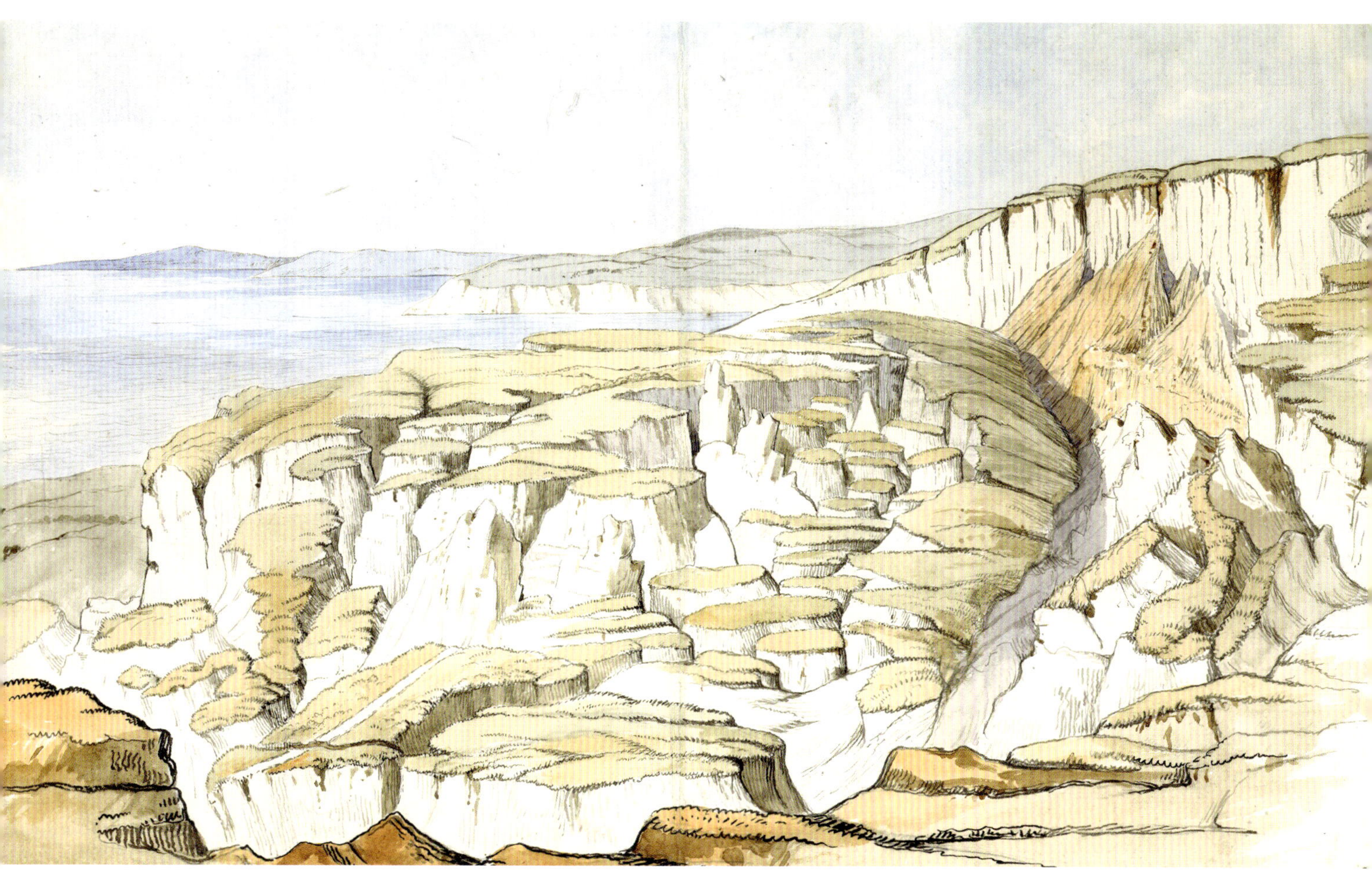

Samuel Palmer RWS Hon. RE • 1805-1881
Harvest in the Vineyard

1859 • watercolour and bodycolour on paper • 19.9 x 42.7 cm
Trustees of the Cecil Higgins Art Gallery (The Higgins Bedford)

Palmer is best known today for the work he produced at Shoreham in the 1820s and early 1830s, when he was inspired by the work of William Blake and encouraged by visits from his young friends to portray the Kent village as an earthly paradise.

In 1837 he married Hannah Linnell, and the couple had a lengthy honeymoon in Italy, lasting over two years. In later life, Palmer always hoped that he would be able to go back to Italy, but financial problems and the demands of a growing family made this difficult.

As he was working on this watercolour, Palmer wrote to a fellow artist: 'I am afraid ... there is "no chance" of my coming to Rome, although I wish to see the southern vintages again, and am attempting one or two haunting memories of my travels.' If he were to go again, he said, he would make 'hundreds of outlines of those rock-lifted cities on hills', and of the roads leading up to them where 'white oxen with bended necks drag the vintage wain'.[1] This view of the grape harvest suggests a golden age, when nature produced abundant fruits, and people and animals gathered them together. There are echoes of Edward Calvert's *The Cyder Feast* (p. 45) in the waggon drawn by oxen, and both the waggon and the handcart in the foreground are so heavily laden with ripe grapes that they can barely be propelled along the ground.

1. R. Lister (ed.), *The Letters of Samuel Palmer* (Oxford: Clarendon Press, 1974), vol. I, pp. 546.

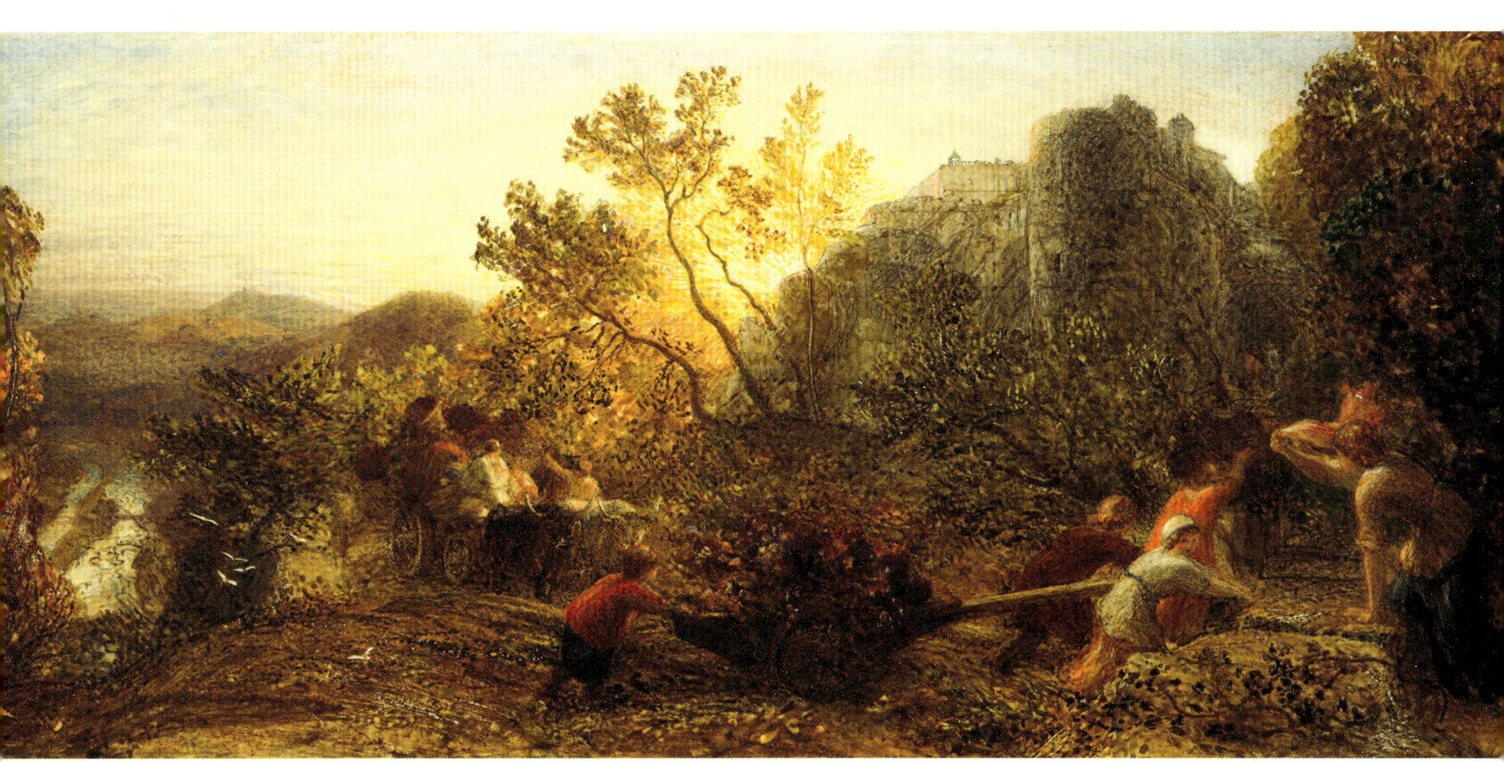

Edward William Cooke RA FRS FZS FSA FGS
1811-1880
Triassic Cliffs, Blue Anchor, North Somerset

1866 • oil on canvas • 42 x 66 cm
Guildhall Art Gallery, City of London

Geology was a subject of passionate debate in the mid-nineteenth century. The examination of rock strata provided evidence that the Earth had been in existence for millions of years, much longer than the time allowed for creation in the biblical account. Moreover, the fossils preserved in those strata were crucial to theories of evolution. Nowhere were the strata more easily observed than at the coast.

Cooke was a successful marine artist. He was also a keen fossil collector and a fellow of the Geological Society of London. The Triassic cliffs at Blue Anchor Bay, near Minehead, were laid down when the area was inundated by shallow seas; their wave-like forms are evidence of powerful natural forces, echoed in the painting in the movements of the clouds and the sea. Although these particular rock formations no longer exist, we may be confident of Cooke's accuracy in his representation of them. He has taken care to show, on the right-hand edge of the canvas, the fault line where the marine sediment of the Penarth Group meets the Red Keuper Marl, which was deposited in a hot desert environment.[1]

Triassic rocks date from the era before the Jurassic, so they are over 200 million years old. The rocks at Blue Anchor Bay contain a thin bone bed which is full of fossilised remains of the reptiles and fish which lived in that remote period, and it is still popular with fossil hunters today.

1. Diana Donald and Jane Munro (eds), *Endless Forms: Charles Darwin, Natural Science and the Visual Arts* (New Haven and London: Yale University Press, 2009), p. 62.

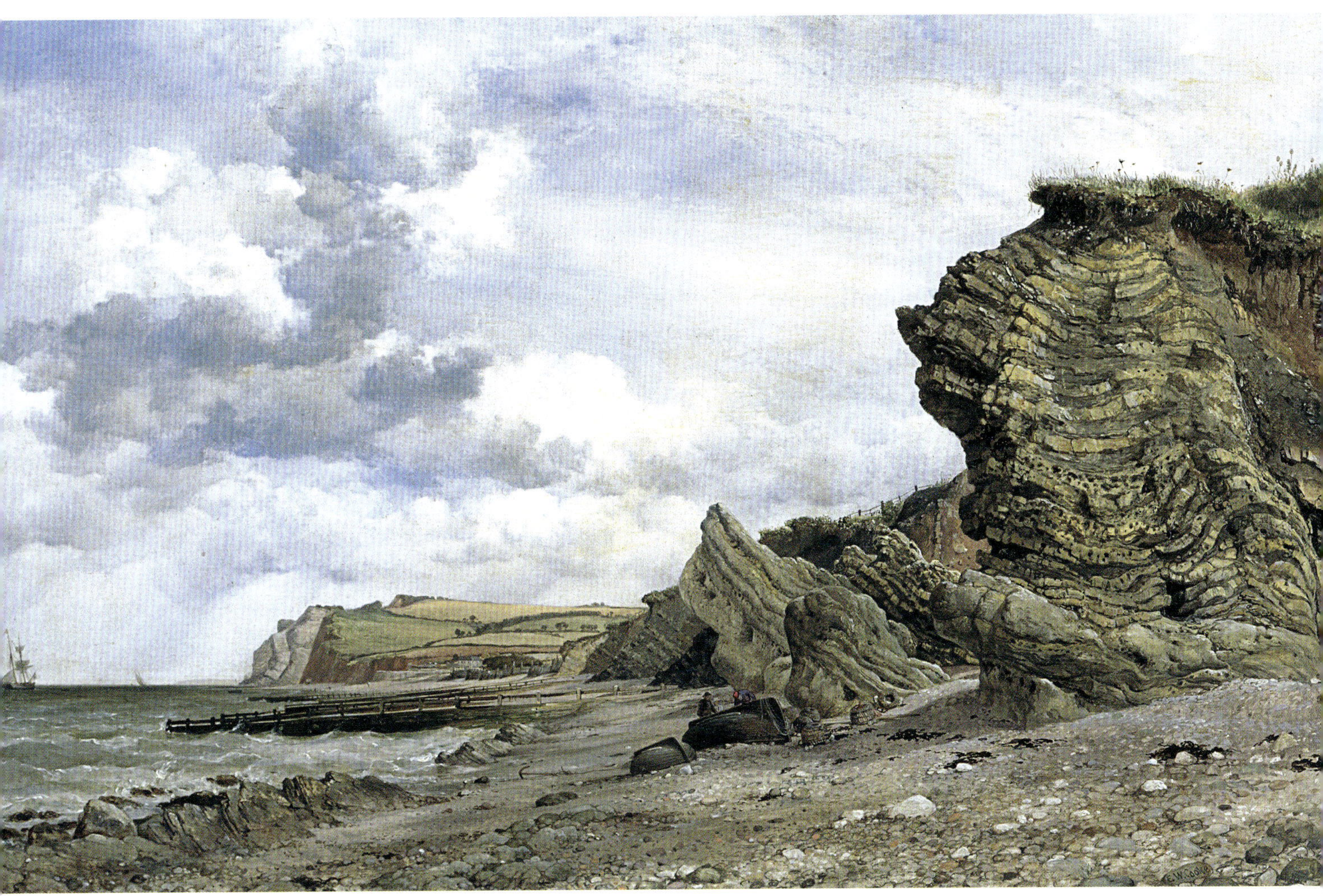

Sir George Clausen RA · 1852-1944
Winter Work

1883-4 · oil on canvas · 77.5 x 92 cm
Tate: purchased with assistance from the Friends of the Tate Gallery, 1983
photo: Tate

In the later decades of the nineteenth century, writers and artists emphasised the harsher aspects of rural life, in a reaction against the idyllic visions that had prevailed in earlier years. The paintings of Jean-François Millet and Jules Bastien-Lepage were shown in London and had a great impact on several British artists, including George Clausen.

In the 1880s Clausen produced a series of paintings of field labourers in Hertfordshire, using photography to help him achieve authenticity in their clothing, poses and physiognomy. They offered a striking contrast to earlier, and even to contemporary, depictions of lively, sunny harvest fields.

In this painting mangold wurzels are being pulled from the ground, covered in soil; thick mud clings to the boots and leggings of the principal figure on the left. Apart from the man's red scarf, the clothes of the labourers share the dull, drab colouring of the earth to which they appear to be bound. The viewer can almost feel the effort that would be required just to walk over the claggy field, let alone to work in it hour after hour.

The picture was exhibited at the Grosvenor Gallery in 1883, but remained unsold. The figure of the girl in a pink dress was added only after the painting came back from the exhibition, presumably in an attempt to lighten the mood and make the work more saleable.[1]

1. Christiana Payne, *Toil and Plenty: Images of the Agricultural Landscape in England, 1780-1890* (New Haven and London: Yale University Press, 1993), p. 126.

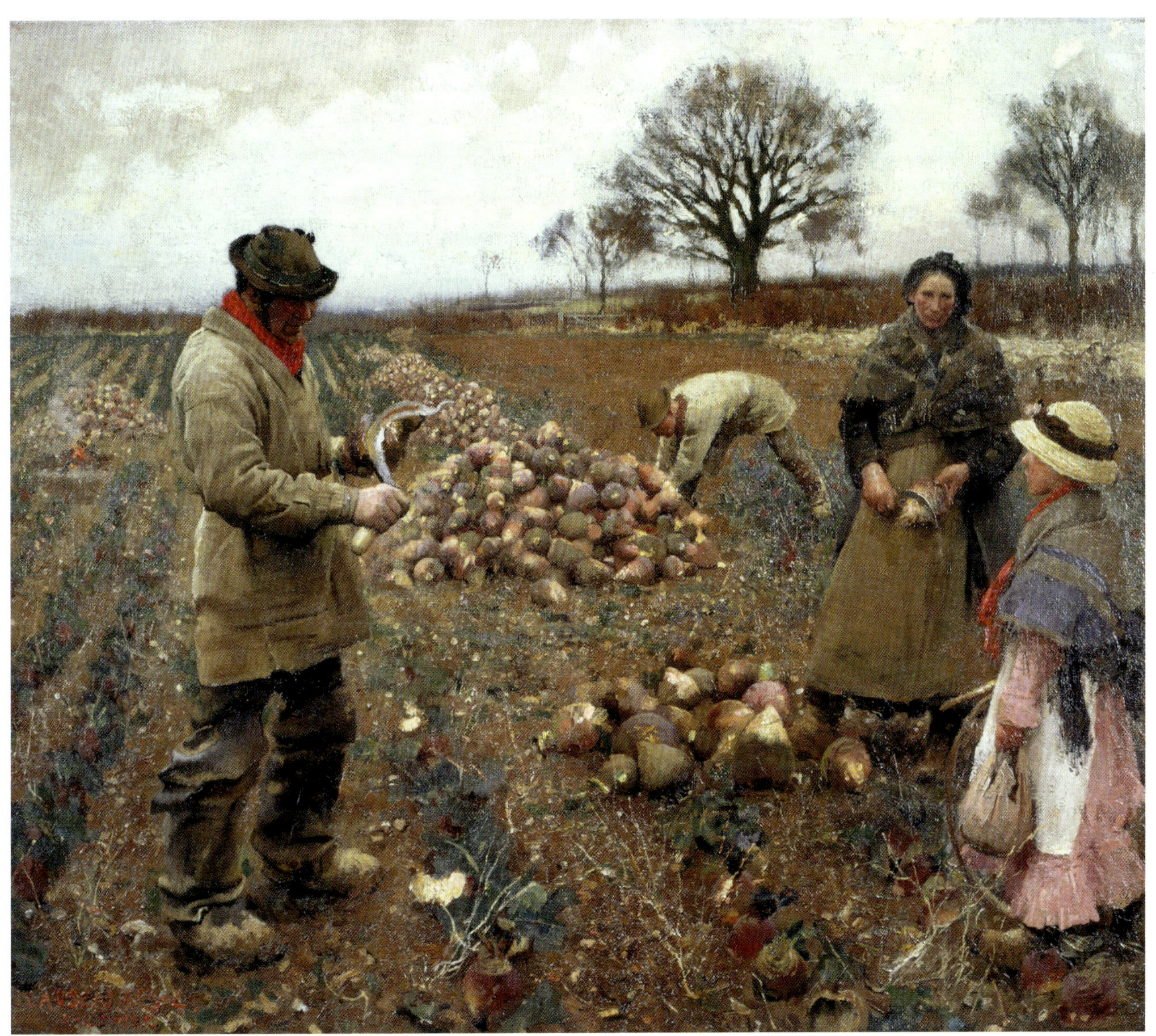

Laura Knight DBE RA RWS · 1877-1970
Men Working in a China Clay Pit

1914 · watercolour and gouache on paper · 50 x 74.5 cm
Penlee House Gallery and Museum, Penzance ·

Having settled in Cornwall in 1907, Knight produced a series of paintings of sunny open-air subjects, such as *The Beach* (*c.* 1909, Laing Art Gallery, Newcastle). In 1914 she and her husband, the artist Harold Knight, were camping out at Dozmary Pool on Bodmin Moor. It was probably then that she visited the huge china clay workings near St Austell, and made a couple of luminous watercolours of men at work in the pits.

By 1910, Cornwall was producing around half the world's china clay (kaolin). Thousands of people worked in the pits and the landscape became dominated by the enormous waste tips that are now known as the Cornish Alps. Today, the St Austell deposits, which have produced around 120 million tonnes of china clay, have been largely abandoned, but their legacy lives on in the Eden Project, which sits in a former clay pit.

With the white clay sides of the pits drenched in sunlight, casting only the palest of blue shadows, Knight's scene looks idyllic. In the centre, the use of high-pressure hoses to remove the clay creates an effect that is similar to traditional renderings of waterfalls. But in reality working conditions were harsh. In 1913 workers had gone on strike, demanding an eight-hour day and higher wages. The dispute politicised the workforce, and when war broke out in 1914 many clay workers refused to volunteer to fight.

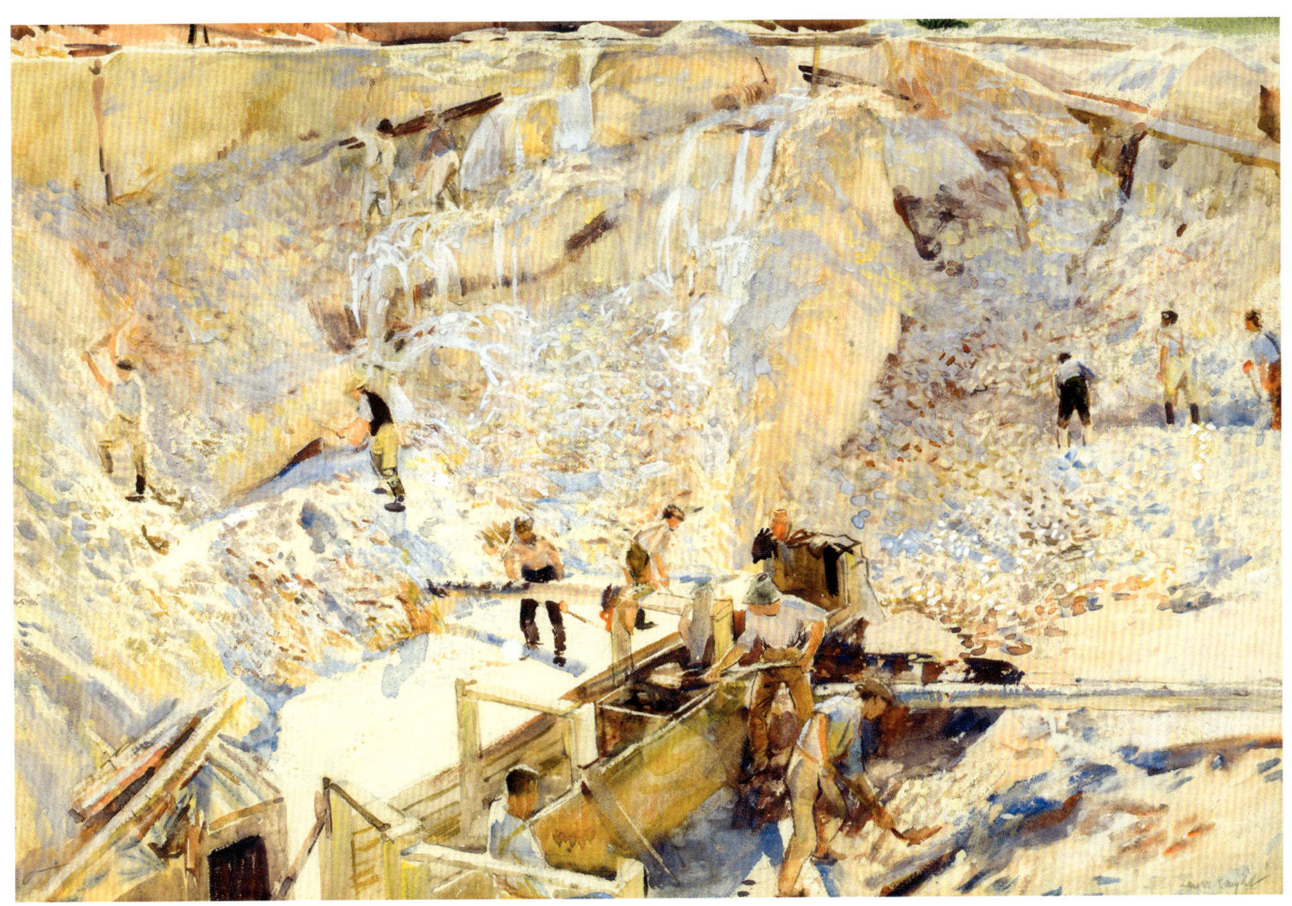

Paul Nash · 1889–1946
Spring in the Trenches, Ridge Wood, 1917

1918 · oil on canvas · 60.9 x 50.8 cm

Nash's war paintings are an eloquent testament to the damage done to the environment, as well as to so many human lives, by the trench warfare of the First World War. This work was a commission from the Ministry of Information, listed as complete in 1918. Before becoming a War Artist, Nash himself had served as an officer in the trenches, and was invalided out just before an attack in which most of the men in his regiment were killed.

In a letter to his wife (7 March 1917), he described a wood on the way to the frontline trenches: 'a place with an evil name, pitted and pocked with shells, the trees torn to shreds, often reeking with poison gas – a most desolate ruinous place two months back, today it was a vivid green; the most broken trees even had sprouted somewhere in the midst, from the depth of the wood's bruised heart poured out the throbbing song of a nightingale. Ridiculous, mad incongruity.'[1]

Natural regeneration is evident in the scene represented here, too: the trees are beginning to produce buds, and there are birds in the brilliantly blue sky. But the exposed earth, carefully depicted in its contrasting colours, is bare and looks naked compared to the neatly dressed soldiers, catching a brief moment of rest and respite before the next onslaught.

1. Imperial War Museums website, https://www.iwm.org.uk/collections/item/object/20079, accessed 10 December 2021.

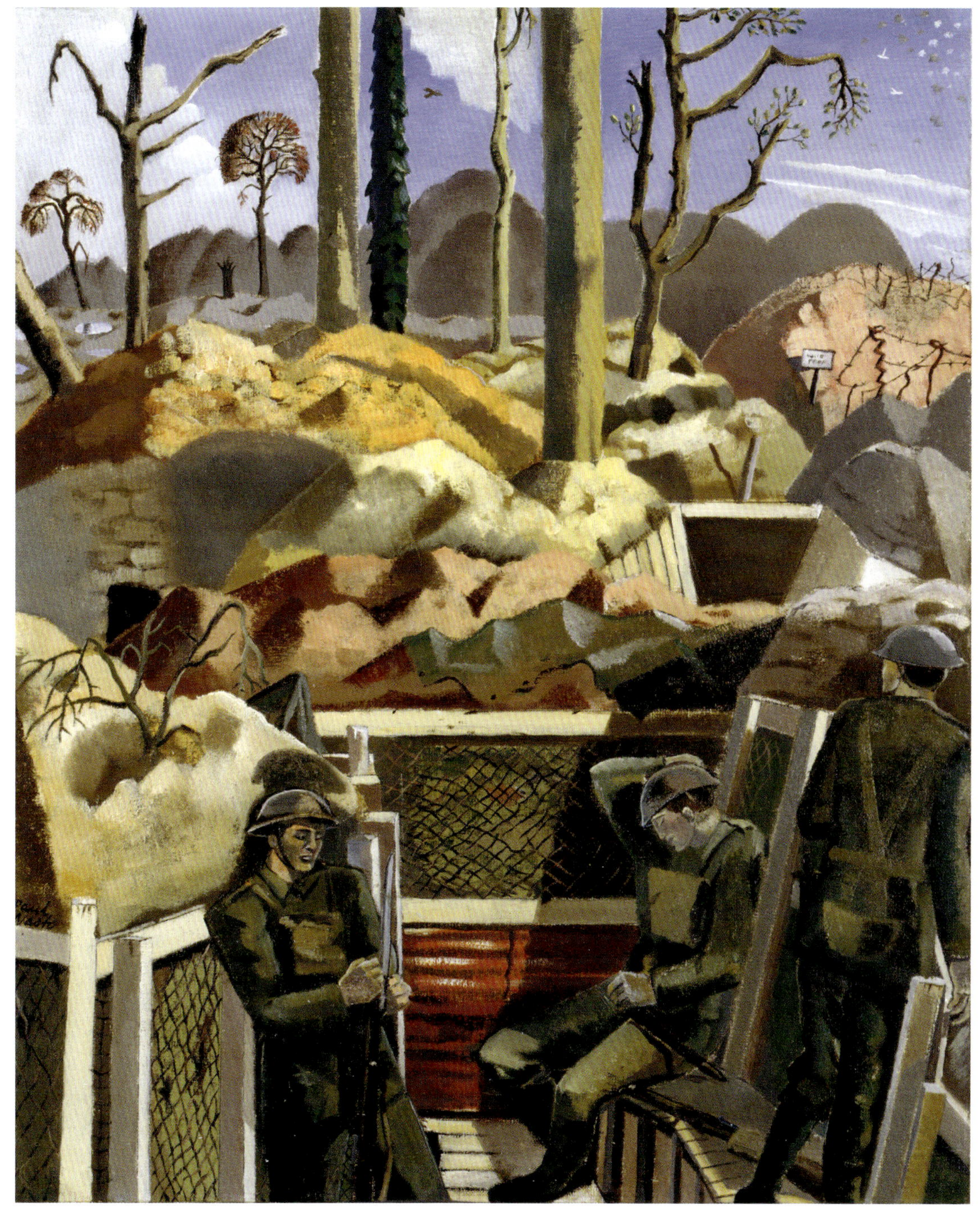

Samuel John Lamorna Birch RA RWS
1869-1955
Morning Fills the Bowl

1926 • oil on canvas • 94.5 x 126 cm
From the collections of the Royal Institution of Cornwall

Birch was a member of the St Ives group of artists, and took his name from the Lamorna valley, where he lived, near Penzance in Cornwall. He was a member of the RWA and was invited to take charge of the hanging of their autumn show in 1922.

Birch enjoyed painting abandoned quarries and clay pits, appreciating the opportunities they presented for depicting reflected light and colour. In this, one of his largest and most dramatic paintings, we look between pillars of granite at the quay and waste tips of the Lamorna Quarry, which had ceased production 15 years earlier. In the centre is the old harbour wall, still with the derrick that was used for loading the stone onto ships.

In the nineteenth century this was the most important quarry in Cornwall, producing granite for, amongst other important projects, the London Embankment. Granite is the hardest stone in the British Isles, and makes up most of the Penwith peninsula, at the far tip of Cornwall. It is responsible for the fine sand and clear seas of the coast there.

The painting was exhibited at the Royal Academy in 1926 and helped to secure Birch's election as ARA. The title refers, not to the granite, but to the luminous sky-reflecting sea: it comes from Edward FitzGerald's nineteenth-century work, *The Rubáiyát of Omar Khayyám*, 'that inverted bowl we call the sky'.[1]

1. Austin Wormleighton, *A Painter Laureate: Lamorna Birch and His Circle* (Bristol: Sansom & Company, 1995), p. 168.

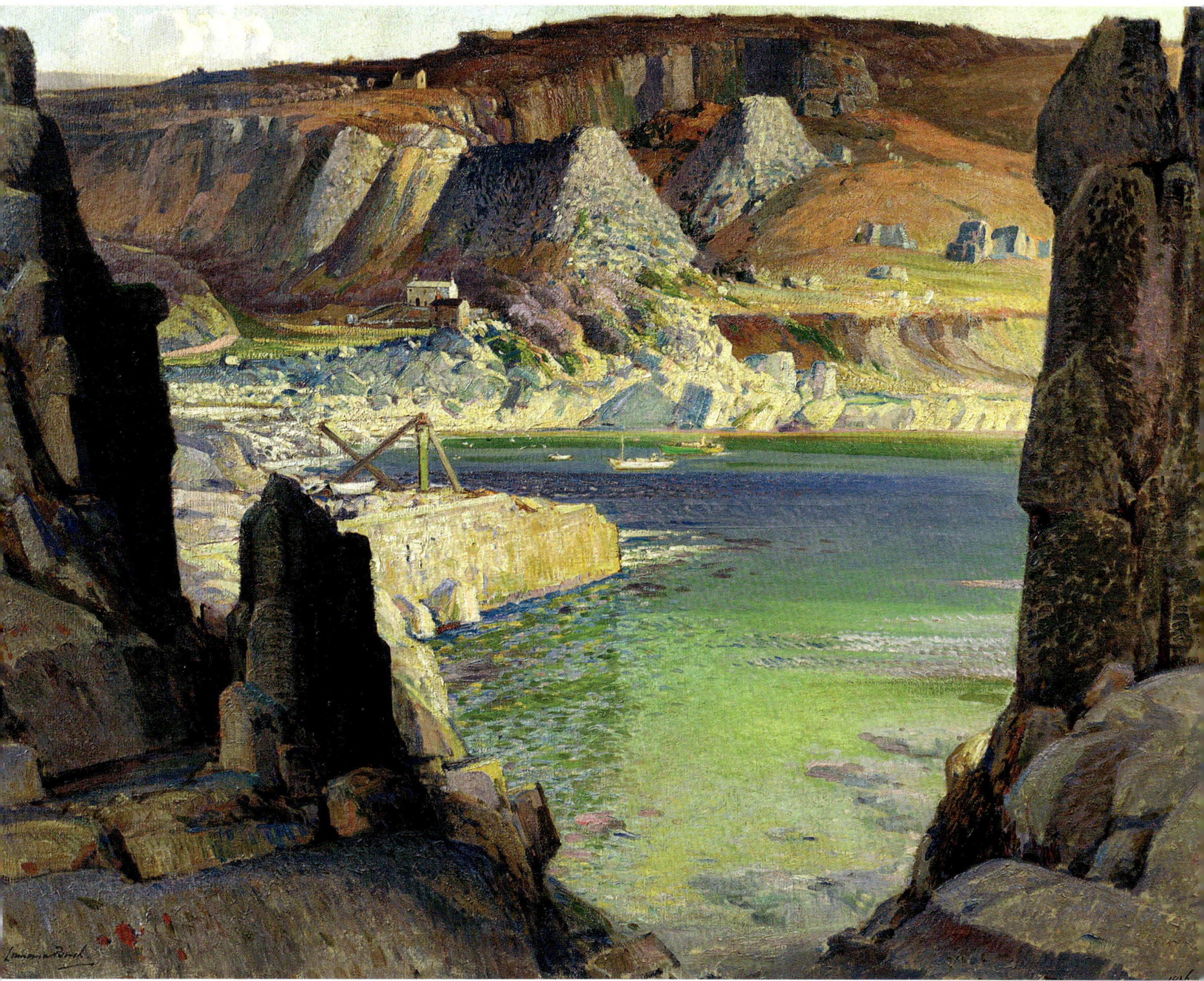

Eric Ravilious · 1903-1942
Downs in Winter

1935 · watercolour on paper · 44.5 x 55.5 cm
Towner Eastbourne

Ravilious grew up near Eastbourne, and explored the South Downs from his boyhood. He was fascinated by the chalk figures that earlier artists had created on the Downs, both in Sussex and in Wiltshire, and in 1939 he produced evocative watercolours of the Long Man of Wilmington, the Uffington White Horse and the Westbury White Horse.

In 1934 he was staying at a cottage, Furlongs, rented by his friend, the artist and designer Peggy Angus. It lies on a track that runs along the base of Beddington Hill near Glynde, at the foot of the South Downs. The next-door neighbour was a ploughman, Mr Barnes, and it is his set of Cambridge rolls that we see in *Downs in Winter*.[1] In other watercolours Ravilious depicted Barnes with horses and waggons, working the land, but here the implement stands in for him, and for the human presence in the landscape generally. Cambridge rolls are used to compact the earth after ploughing, harrowing and sowing.

Ravilious loved the wide open spaces of the downs, and the way the chalky earth is exposed, either in the chalk figures or in the paths across the fields. He even painted the local chalk quarry and cement works, with its chalk-whitened buildings. In this watercolour the earth looks bleak and bare, but the roller tells us that it has been planted with seedcorn, ready to 'green up' in the coming spring.

1. James Russell, *Eric Ravilious: Downland Man* (Devizes: Wiltshire Archaeological and Natural History Society, 2021), p. 17.

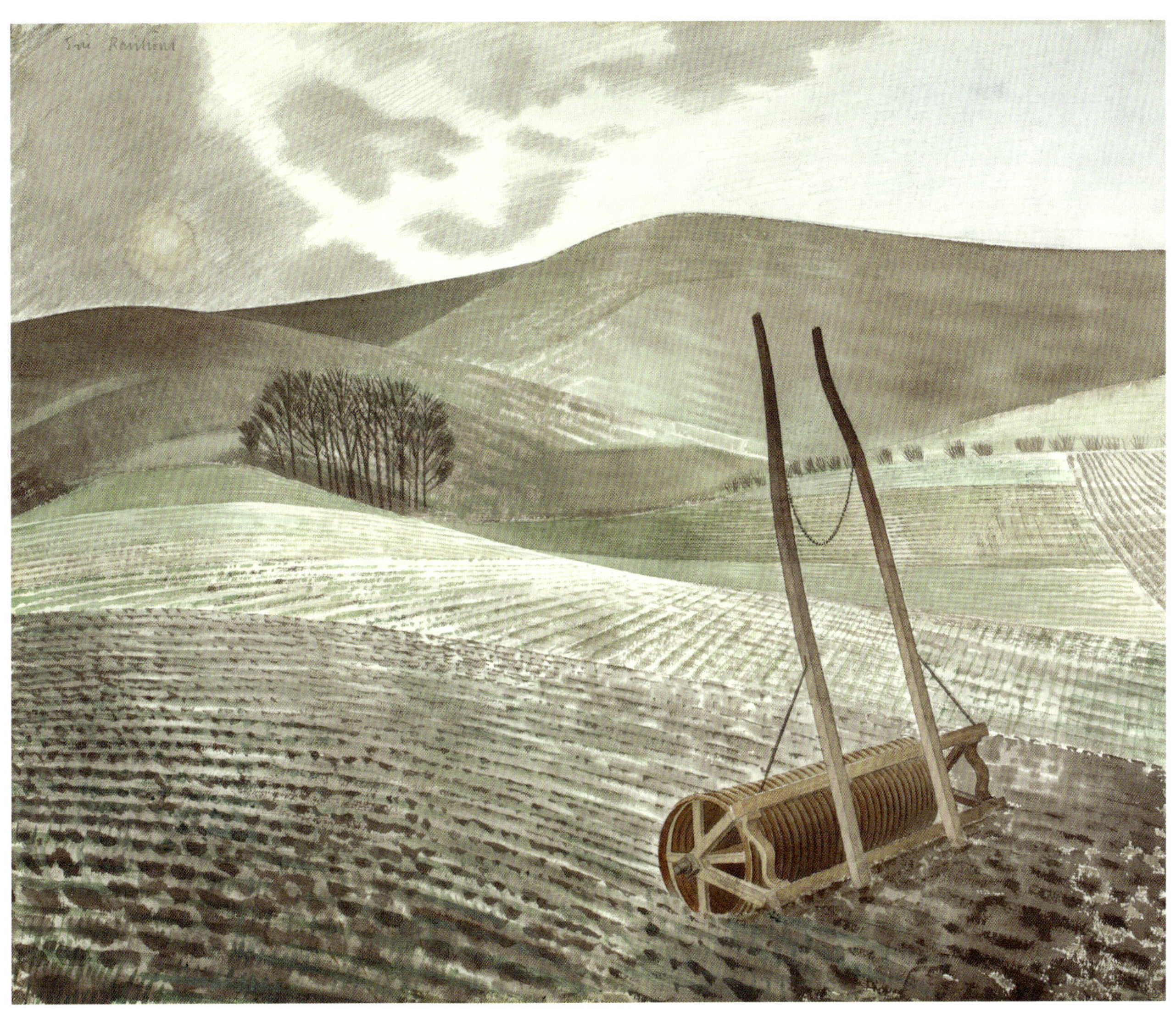
Eric Ravilious

Stanley Spencer CBE RA · 1891-1959

Rickett's Farm, Cookham Dene

1938 · oil on canvas · 66 x 116.8 cm

Tate: purchased 1938 · · photo: Tate

Spencer was born in the village of Cookham in Berkshire, and spent most of his life there. To him it was a 'village in Heaven', and one of his most famous paintings, *The Resurrection, Cookham* (1924–7, Tate), represents it as a site of the miraculous. Cookham Dean, or Dene, is an adjoining hamlet, more rural than its neighbour.

In 1938, Spencer painted 19 landscape and still-life paintings between 13 February and 10 August. He found painting landscapes difficult and slow, and regarded it as an obstacle to his figurative work, but he needed to make money. The landscapes sold well: their lush sensuousness and pastoral subjects appealed to those who were nostalgic for the rural life of the cottage, the farm and the village, and they were seen as carrying on the tradition of Constable, Palmer and the Pre-Raphaelites. This painting was sold to the Tate Gallery in the year it was painted.[1]

The foreground subject of pigs sets an 'earthy' tone: the baby piglets on the right scramble over one another as they try to reach their mother's teats, and one of the older piglets on the left has just had a piddle. A muckheap, a strip of bare earth and a row of cabbages lie just beyond the pigpen. Hayricks in the middle distance, trees dotted with fruit, and chicken sheds on the right all contribute to the overall impression of a countryside teeming with growth and productiveness.

1. Keith Bell, *Stanley Spencer: A Complete Catalogue of the Paintings* (London: Phaidon Press Ltd, in association with Christie's and the Henry Moore Foundation, 1992), pp. 278, 284.

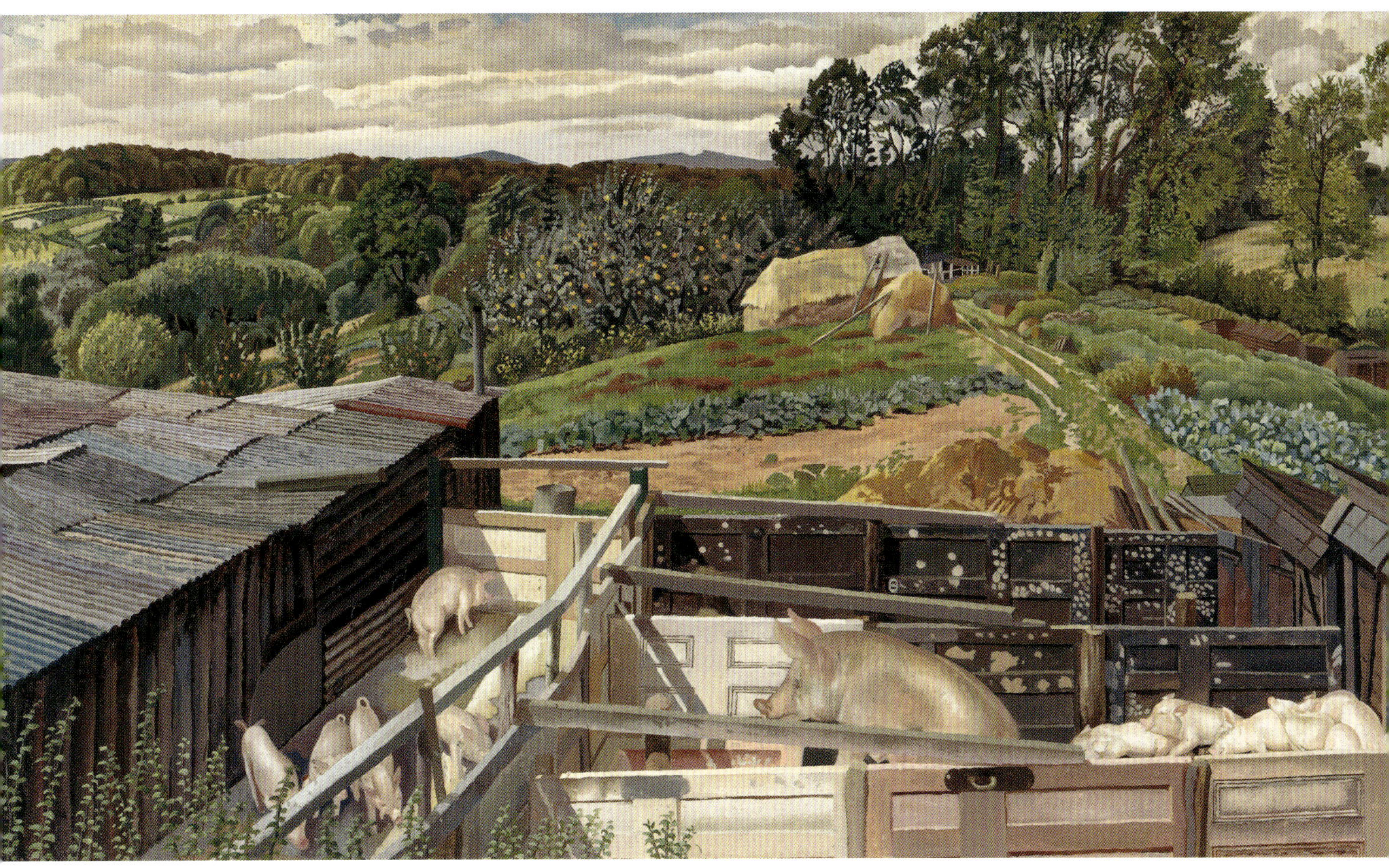

Graham Sutherland OM · **1903-1980**
Cornish Tin Mine, Emerging Miner

1943 · oil on canvas · 118.1 x 76.2 cm

In June 1943, Sutherland, as an official war artist, spent three weeks working in the Geevor tin mine near Penzance in Cornwall. The war had created a severe scarcity of tin, so its production was a major priority, and skilled miners were hard to find. Sutherland went down the mine in the mornings with a small sketchbook, and worked up his studies in the afternoons.

While he was working there, Sutherland wrote to Kenneth Clark: 'The mines are stupendous & thrilling to a degree which I wouldn't have believed possible & life below is awe-inspiring ...'[1] He annotated one of his studies for this work as follows: 'Suggest miner in distance coming round curve of stope [the area from which the tin is being mined] (very strong feeling of shut-in-ness and weight of stone). Miner emerges from entrance of stope. Very mysterious. Approach associated with noise of boots and falling stones and with approaching light of lamp. Remember light flesh colour derived from light reflected from close walls.'[2]

In 1971 he recalled his experiences in the mine. He described being put through 'hair-raising tests' to test his nerve: being taken down on a bucket holding onto a rope, descending 1,300 feet 'like a bullet' and then being made to go down a ladder in total darkness. In order to function, he had to overcome his claustrophobia, and in the 'endless' passages he marked his way with chalk on the walls so that he would not get lost.[3]

1. Paul Gough, Sally Moss and Tehmina Goskar, *Graham Sutherland: From Darkness into Light. Mining, Metal and Machines* (Bristol: Sansom & Company, 2012), p. 19.
2. Ronald Alley, *Graham Sutherland* (London: Tate Gallery, 1982), p. 99.
3. Martin Hammer, *Graham Sutherland: Landscapes, War Scenes, Portraits 1924–1950* (London: Scala Publishers, 2005), p. 104.

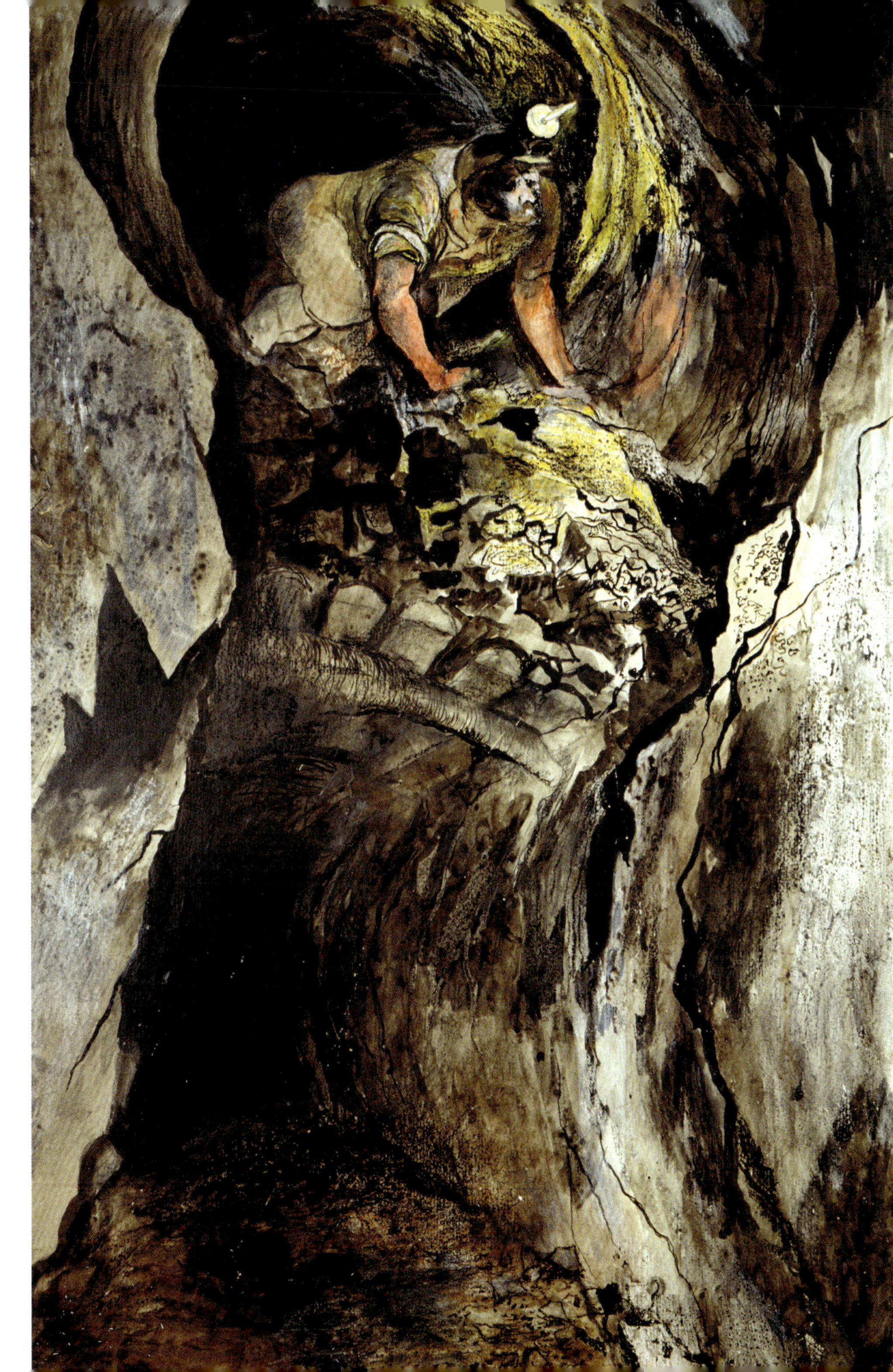

John Piper CH · 1903-1992
Weathercote Cave

1943 · oil on canvas · 63.5 x 45.7 cm

Southwark Art Collection/Southwark Council and South London Gallery

In the early 1940s John Piper was collecting illustrated books from the late eighteenth and early nineteenth centuries, and visiting the 'picturesque' and 'sublime' sites that had been recorded by artists such as Richard Wilson, J.M.W. Turner and James Ward. Weathercote Cave, in Yorkshire, is a rocky chasm with an eighty-foot waterfall at its far end. A large piece of stone is wedged across the gully at the top end of the waterfall. Turner painted a watercolour of the cave in around 1816, for an illustration in Thomas Whitaker's *History of Richmondshire*. Piper took the same viewpoint, focusing more narrowly on the waterfall and its surrounding rock, and depicting it in bright, vibrant colours.

The cave was first drawn to the public's attention in 1780 by John Hutton, who described it as 'the most surprising natural curiosity in the island of Great Britain'. A century later John Ruskin declared that it was 'the rottenest – deadliest – loveliest – horriblest place I ever saw in my life'.[1] Piper used this painting as the basis for a lithograph, which was reproduced in *English, Scottish and Welsh Landscapes* (1944).

1. Thomas West, *A Guide to the Lakes* (London: Richardson and Urquhart, 1780), pp. 253-5; E.T. Cook and A. Wedderburn (eds), *The Works of John Ruskin* (London: George Allen, 1903-12), vol. 37, p. 181.

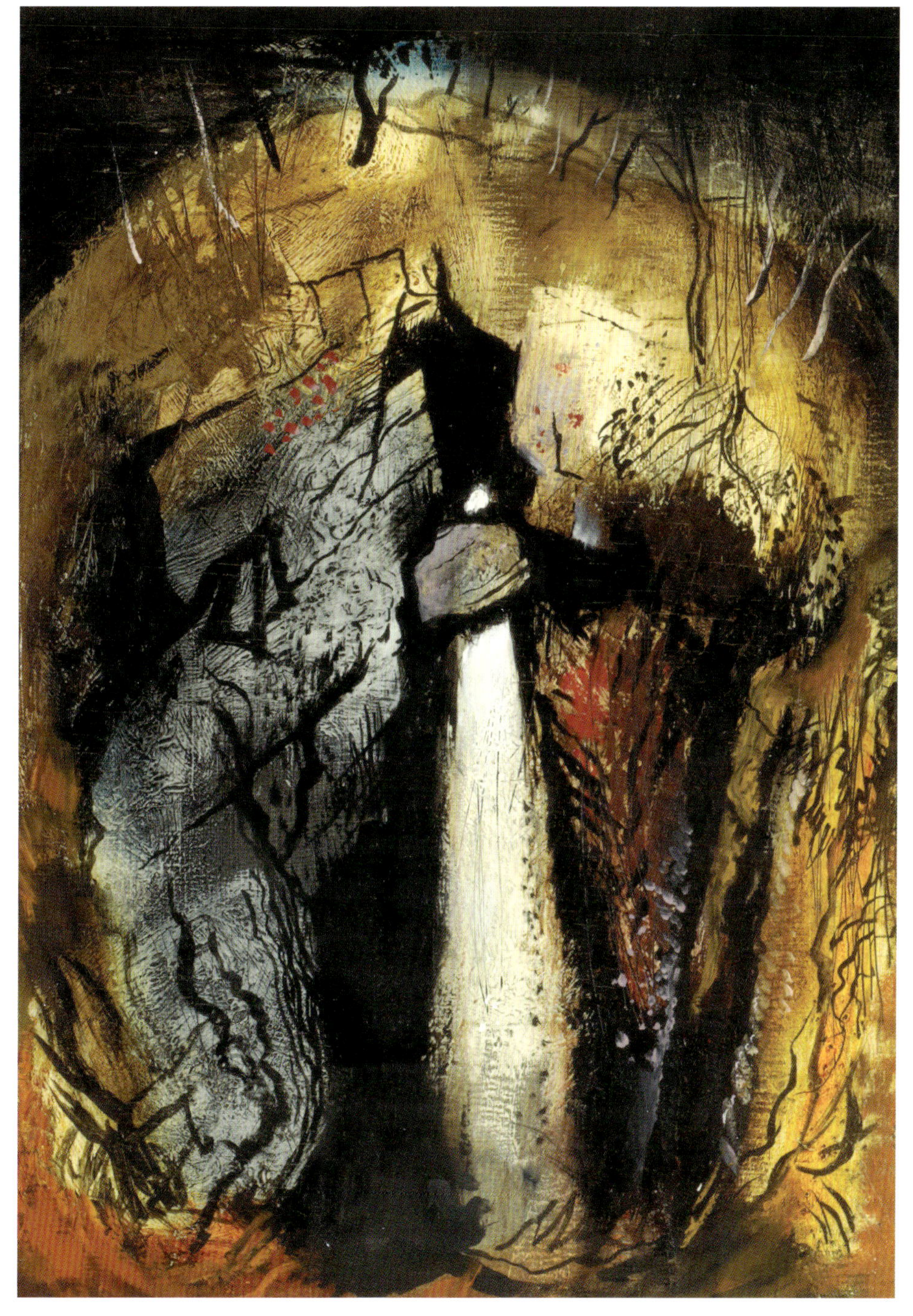

John Nash CBE RA · 1893-1977
Landscape near Hadleigh

*c.*1945 · watercolour and gouache on paper · 36.8 x 52.2 cm

Harlow Council: gift of Sir Frederick Gibberd, 1981 •

John Nash was the younger brother of Paul Nash. He served in the First World War and became an official war artist, like his brother, in 1918. After the war, he painted landscapes and botanical illustrations, and became an accomplished printmaker.

From 1944 he lived, with his wife Christine, at Bottengoms Farmhouse near Wormingford in Essex, on the edge of the Stour Valley landscapes made famous by John Constable. In the spring and the summer they would travel to other parts of Britain, but in winter, his favourite season as an artist, Nash painted in his much-loved garden and in the area near his house. The market town of Hadleigh is about half an hour's drive from Wormingford.

In the later 1940s, 1950s and 1960s, Nash painted a succession of watercolours of everyday subjects, especially ponds and rivers, trees and fields. At one point he wrote to his great friend, Ronald Blythe: 'You know I never look for more than the reality, the farming, the trees, the river. I suppose the poetry gets into the reality.'[1]

In this watercolour the ploughed field, with its curving lines, is so fluid that it almost takes on the appearance of water. The fresh earth is ready for planting, and the bare trees glisten in the sunlight, offering a promise of the coming spring.

1. Andy Friend, *John Nash: The Landscape of Love and Solace* (London: Thames & Hudson, 2020), p. 271.

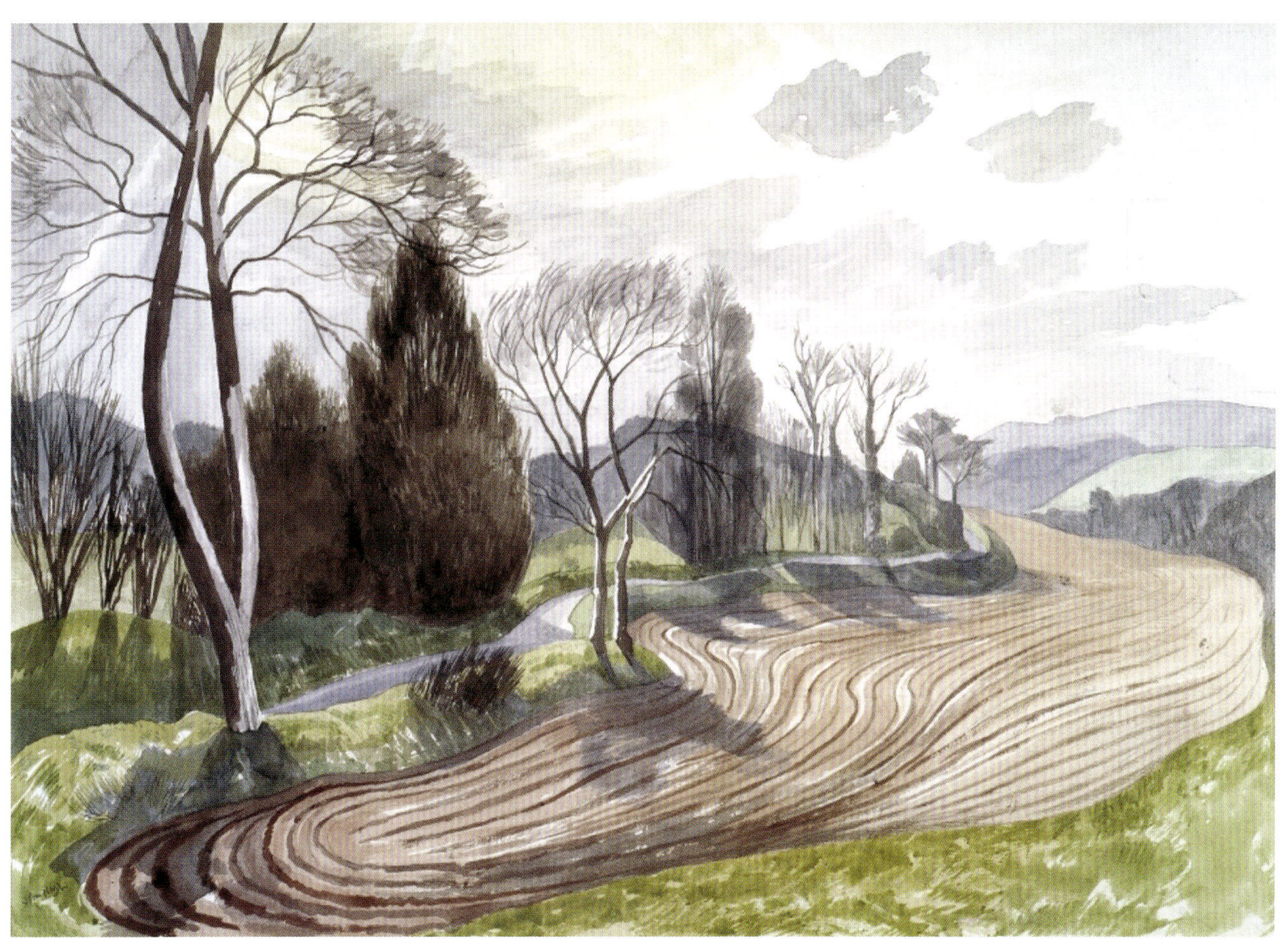

Wilhelmina Barns-Graham

CBE RWA Hon RSA Hon RSW Hon · 1912–2004

Glacier, Rock Forms

1950 · oil on canvas · 51 x 76 cm

Wolverhampton Art Gallery ·

On a holiday in Switzerland in 1949, Barns-Graham visited the Grindelwald glaciers. The drawings and watercolours she made on site provided material for a whole series of glacier paintings, which gradually became more abstract.

She later recalled that she was enthralled by the 'massive strength and size of the glaciers, the fantastic shapes, the contrast of solidity and transparency, the many reflected colours in strong light, the warmth of the sun changing and melting the forms … a piece could disintegrate and fall off, breaking the silence with a sharp crack and its echoes. It seemed to Breathe! Enormous standing forms, polished like glass with sharp edges, … buried in it and on it, huge and tiny stones and rubble …'

She said that in her paintings she had wanted to combine all the angles at once 'from above, through, and all round, as a bird flies, a total experience'.[1] In the last seven words of this passage she was self-consciously quoting Naum Gabo, whose work was an important source of inspiration for her.

The visit to Grindelwald was a turning point in Barns-Graham's life. Since 1940, she had been producing abstracts, but had kept them hidden. The exploration of form she pursued in her glacier paintings gave her the courage she needed to become a purely abstract artist.

1. Letter from artist to Tate Gallery, 1965, cited in Lynne Green, *W. Barns-Graham: A Studio Life* (London: Lund Humphries, 2001), p. 105.

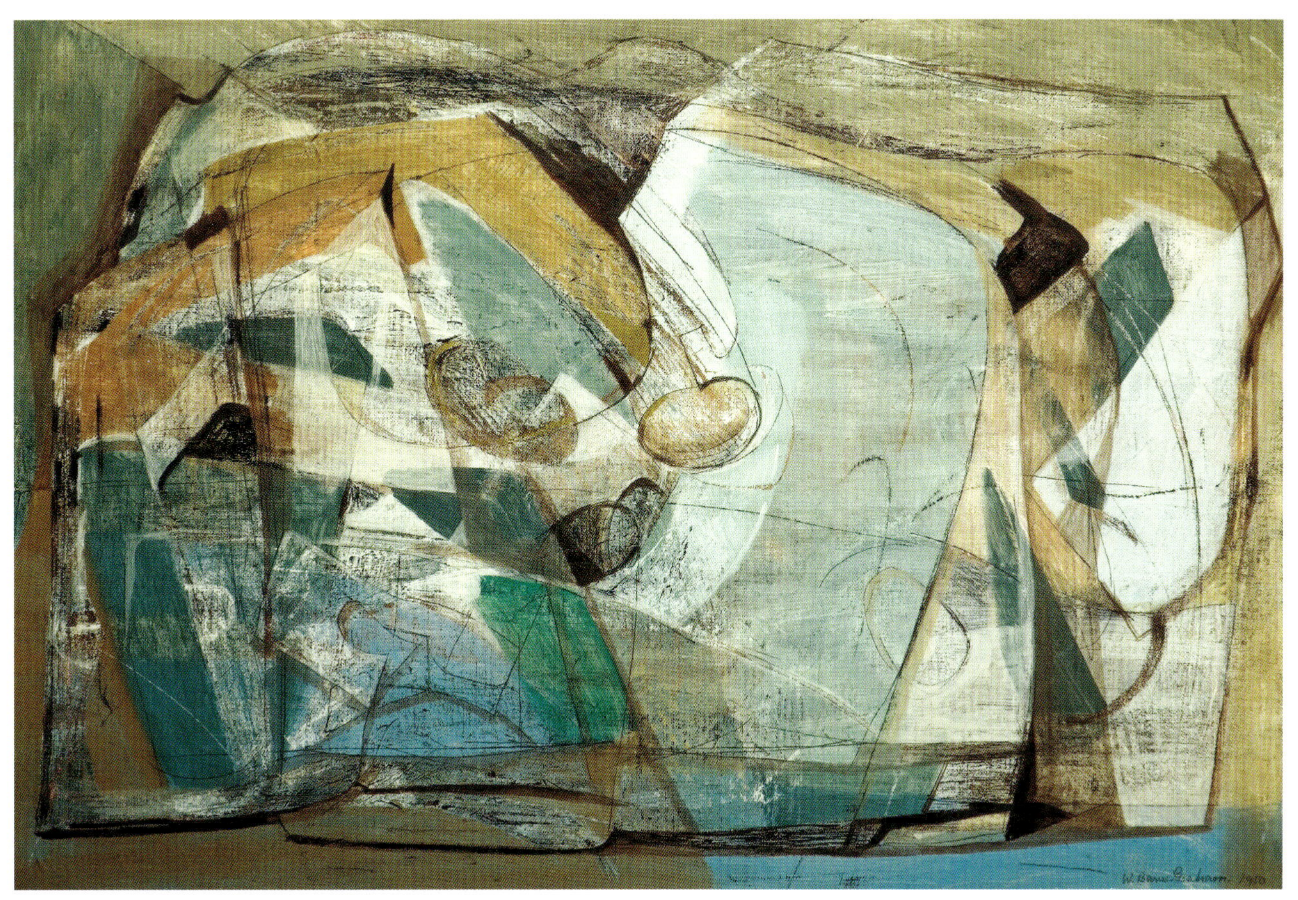

Claude Rogers · 1907-1979
The Combine

1953 · oil on canvas · 91 x 75.5 cm
RWA Collection • © Crispin Rogers • photograph RWA

Nineteenth-century artists enjoyed depicting bustling harvest fields full of men and women, cutting and binding the stalks of wheat so that they could dry out before being taken to a barn for further processing. In the 1950s, however, the harvesting jobs formerly done by hand – reaping, setting up stooks, loading waggons and threshing – could now be done in a single operation with a combine harvester. Only one worker was needed to drive the combine; corn carts would receive the grain periodically and transport it to a dryer.

Rogers may have thought his harvest field would look too lonely with the combine alone, so he has added two further figures: the man talking to the combine driver could be the farmer, discussing a problem with the machinery, while the man with the dog may be out for a walk. The stooks on the right contribute additional pictorial interest to the scene, and imply that the older practices were still being used alongside the new. The high horizon, the bright colours and the expressive brushstrokes show the artist's indebtedness to Vincent Van Gogh, who had also loved painting the wheat harvest.

The artist was a founding member of the Euston Road School in 1937 and became one of the leading upholders of the figurative tradition in British art. He taught at the Camberwell and Slade art schools and the University of Reading.

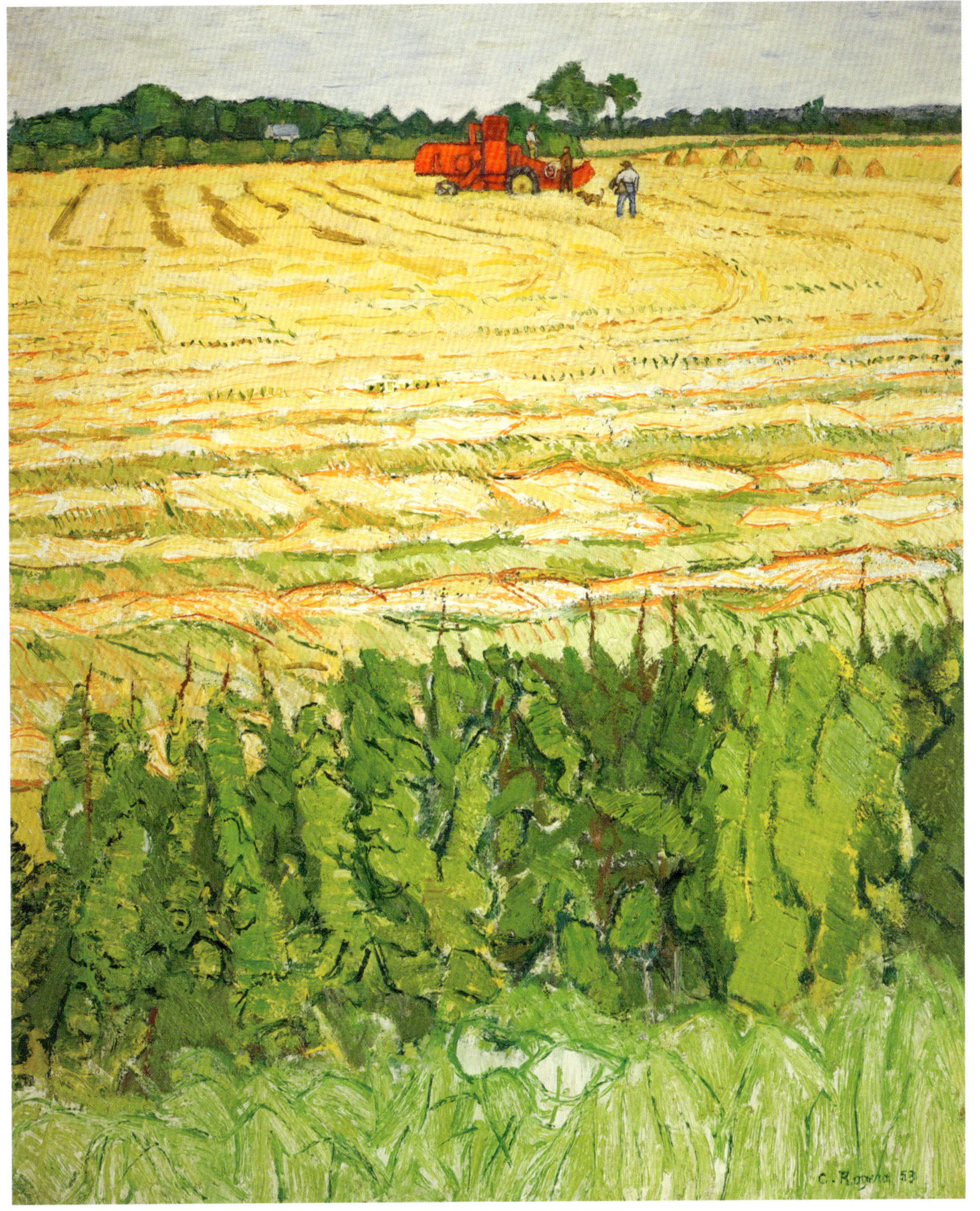

Anthony Gross CBE RA · 1905-1984
Grape Harvest (Vendanges)

1972 · etching on paper · 27.5 x 33.6 cm
Trustees of the Cecil Higgins Art Gallery (The Higgins Bedford)

As a young man, Gross trained in London, Paris and Madrid, and painted in Spain and Brussels. He became a war artist in the Second World War, accompanying the D-Day landings and witnessing the devastation caused by the war in northern France.

Gross was trained as a printmaker by W.P. Robins, author of *Etching Craft* (1922), who advised his pupils to use the burin 'like a spider crawling around'.[1] Gross himself became Head of Department (Etching and Engraving) at the Slade School of Fine Art (1955–71). He was a great observer of people, and his prints are notable for the lively interest they show in everyday activities.

In 1955 Gross bought a house at Le Boulvé, a small village in hill country in south-west France, not far from Montauban. After his retirement from the Slade he used to go there to draw and paint every summer, always working directly from nature. He made several etchings of grape picking, relishing the abstract shapes made by the vine leaves. In this print, the work does not look easy, with most of the figures shown bending over or kneeling on the ground, while the young woman carrying the basket seems exhausted by her labours. Yet the large areas of bare earth in the foreground, set off against generous clusters of grapes, serve to emphasise the richness of the soil and the productiveness of the crowded fields.

1. Cited in Anthony Gross, *Etching, Engraving and Intaglio Printing* (London: Oxford University Press, 1970), p. 55.

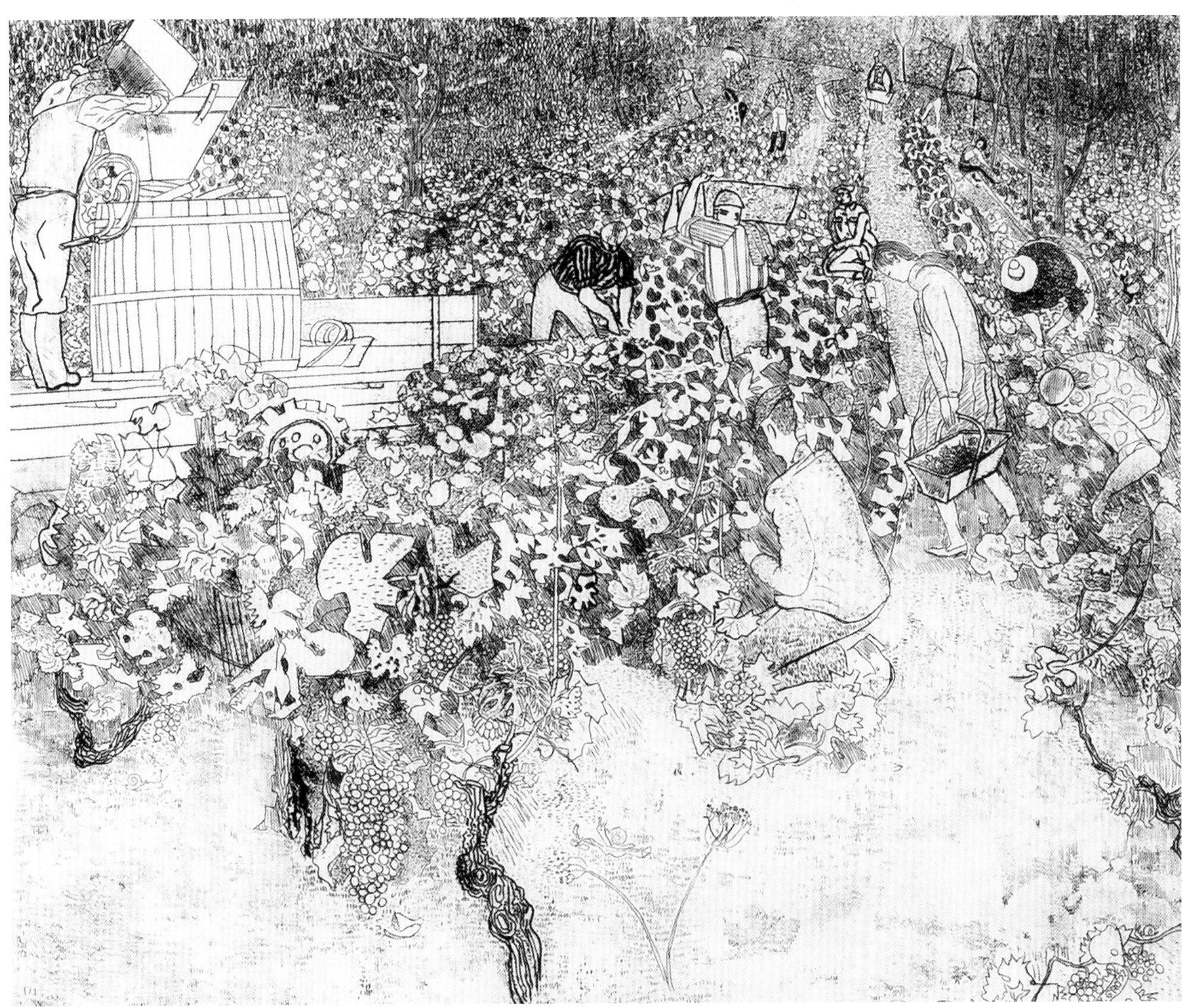

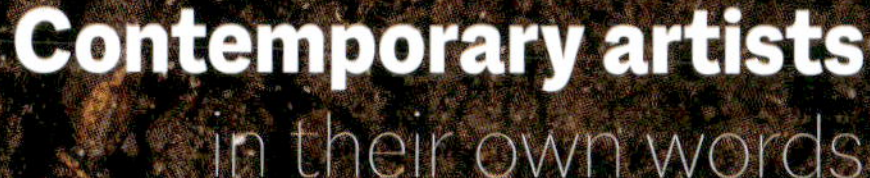
Contemporary artists
in their own words

Edward Chell
Medway Services M20 Eastbound

The Garden of England series • 2013 • oil on shellac on linen • 180 x 140 cm
courtesy the artist • reprinted with kind permission
 • exhibition view Chisenhale Gallery, London

Medway Services M20 Eastbound is part of a series of paintings documenting and exploring threshold bands of landscape that are rarely experienced in the still. The Highways Agency describe these ribbons of green as their 'Soft Estate' – a revel of wild vegetation, litter, hardcore and sometimes rare species – acting as a frame to the landscapes beyond, usually experienced at high speed and untouchable. They have even been described as 'Britain's largest unofficial nature reserve', acting as connective corridors for species. We often pass them by unnoticed. These edgelands are contested ground depending on how you view them with land access campaigner Marion Shoard saying, 'we may not notice it, but it is here that much of our current environmental change ... is taking place' in spite of which 'edgelands have become the lowest grade of landscape in UK landscape conservation terms ... It is time for the edgelands to get the recognition that Emily Brontë and William Wordsworth brought to the moors and mountains and John Betjeman to the suburbs. They too have their story. It is the more cogent and urgent for being the story of our age.'[1]

1. Marion Shoard, 'Edgelands', in Jennifer Jenkins, ed., *Remaking the Landscape: The Changing Face of Britain* (London: Profile Books, 2002), pp. 117–46, see also http://www.marionshoard.co.uk/Documents/Articles/Environment/Edgelands-Remaking-the-Landscape.pdf and https://www.slideshare.net/henningthomsen/edgelands-remakingthelandscape.

Alice Cunningham
preparatory cut-out from sketch book

2022 • 13 x 11 cm
courtesy the artist

Our relationship with earth has always intrinsically been linked to our health. With humans' rapid expansion, demands and modernisation the delicacy and complexity of this fragile relationship is under immense pressure.

With this exhibition, we are provided with an opportunity to look at the dynamics of this throughout history and art-making. Art being a very relevant lens with which to discuss this relationship, as through artworks we not only see representations but also aspirations and emotional responses to the environment we inhabit.

Using disappearing islands, slumping earth and crumbling coastlines as inspiring visual references. In this new body of work I want to explore the material fragility of our environment and the pressure it comes under while still celebrating its resilience and boundless potential.

I find all of these concepts rich to discuss visually and create discussion around. As is commonly the way that our relationship to our surroundings and how we engage in the natural world often manifests as a reflection of what is happening to us internally or as a society.

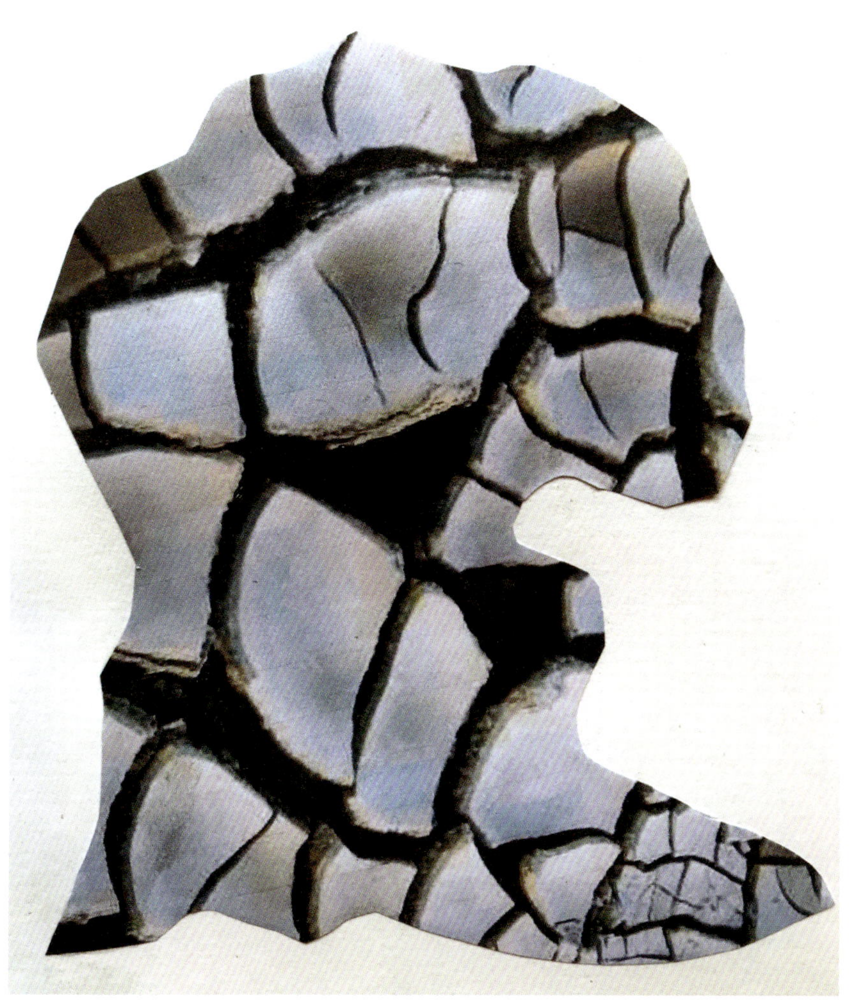

Dalziel + Scullion RSA
Immersion Clothing: Silhouette, Rain, Recumbent, Gatherer

2014 • Harris Tweed
courtesy the artists

This work continued to explore an idea that penetrates many of our artworks – the creation of catalytic objects that have the potential to shift perception of everyday things. Here a series of garments focus the wearer on actions that are powerful immersive acts. Four garments evolved into a 'family' of wearers that spans three generations and contrast with the usual purpose of outdoor clothing that shield and protect and, by extension, isolate the wearer.

Silhouette was worn by the elder of the family, allowing the wearer to shape-shift their form from that of a human to something more akin to an erratic boulder. *Rain* was worn by the child of the group, allowing the wearer to experience rain directly and luxuriously, rearranging the notion of 'dressing for the outdoors'.

The *Recumbent Jacket* is a wearable form of a previous work we made called Rosnes Bench. Here the wearer is encouraged to go out and seek a place to lie down, perhaps somewhere tree canopies or skies can be observed. When no longer on your feet, the surrounding acoustics can seem to increase in volume and allow other nuanced stimulants to be perceived. It encourages the wearer to suspend inhibition and become immersed in a landscape.

Finally, the *Gatherer Jacket* adopted tailoring details from traditional men's suits where pockets would be cut just deep enough for specific things like combs, train tickets or spectacles; in this jacket the pockets were tailored around eye loupes, glass vials and for collating field findings and cuttings. With specific pockets to fill, it gives the wearer an agenda to go out into a landscape, with their eyes that bit keener, their level of interest no longer passive.

This family of garments usher in a restrained sort of resistance toward our overly domesticated lives and perhaps the agency to go out of doors with a renewed purpose, allowing encounters with Nature to become more intimate and revelatory.

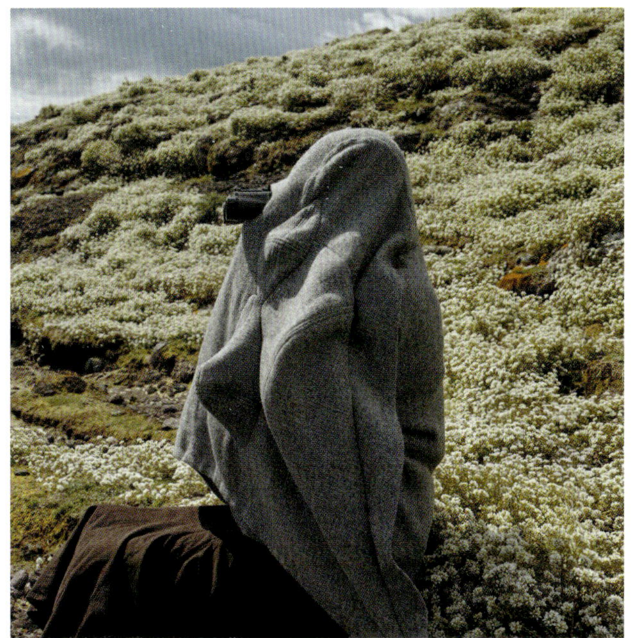

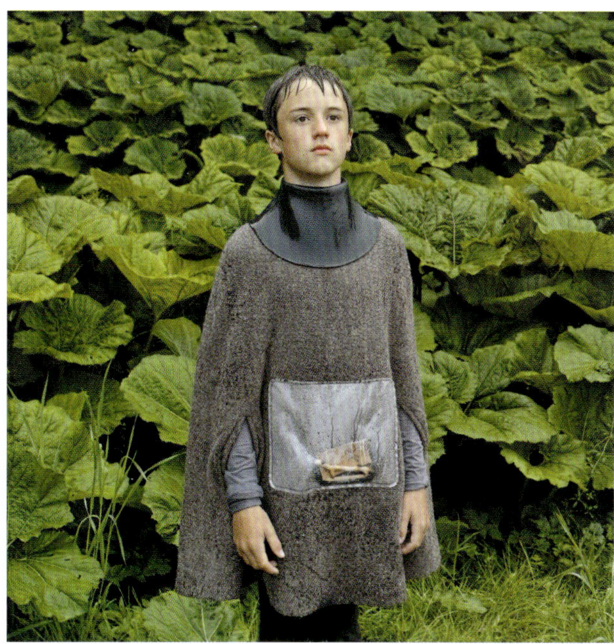

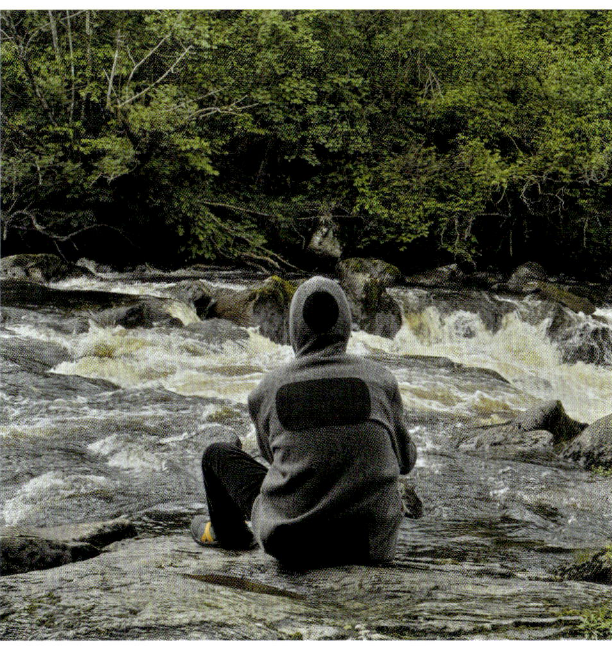

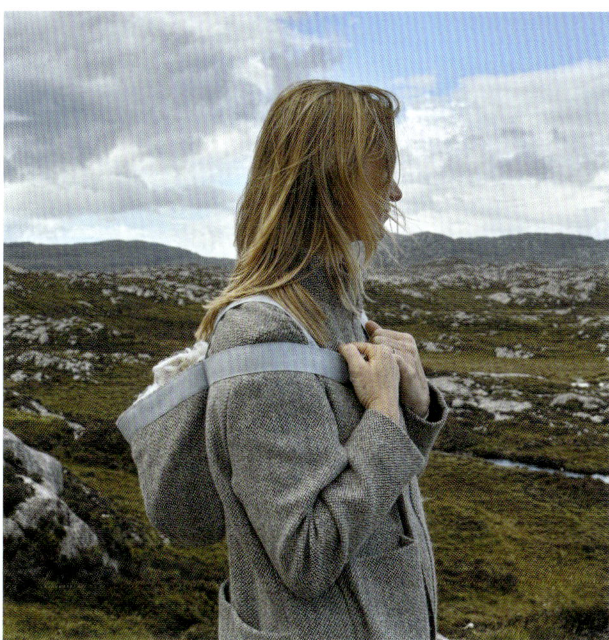

Susan Derges RWA Hon
Shoreline

2018 • polymer photogravure with chine-collé, hand-painted, edition of six with + two APs • 92 x 156 cm

In the late 1990s I made many photographic prints of sea waves rolling onto Devon beaches and across light sensitive paper that I had placed in their path, at night, when the landscape became a huge darkroom and there was no danger of fogging the paper. The results were extraordinarily detailed and expressive of the conditions of each particular moment and yet they seemed to read ambiguously, taking on some of the shapes and lines familiar from satellite images of the Earth's surface, where land meets ocean or in the fluid movements of cloud and weather fronts. The microcosm seems to map onto the macrocosm perfectly in such areas and beyond them into the minutiae of everyday life – ripples in a teacup, light traces in the bath, edges and grain in wood, marble and folds of skin ... The delicate balance of these processes has become more widely appreciated since I first made the prints and I decided to revisit the imagery, and made a series of polymer photogravures in which the preciousness and precariousness of the land/ocean were emphasised by the use of a gold ground and overprinting in deep red/brown.

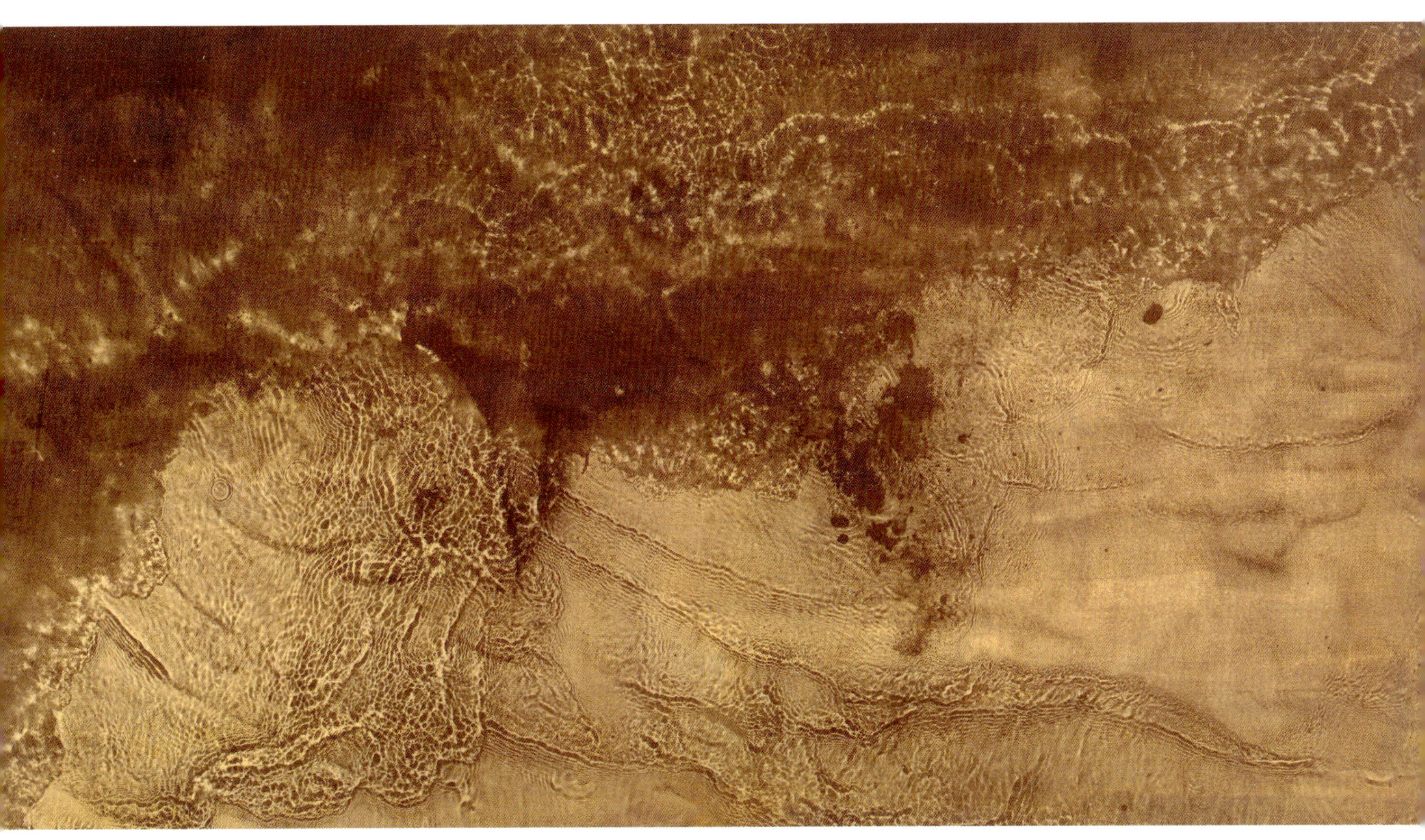

Anya Gallaccio
Untitled

2016 • dirt and mixed pigment on paper • 51 x 60.1 cm
courtesy the artist and Thomas Dane Gallery • © Anya Gallaccio
photograph Lewis Ronald

'Gallaccio employs organic materials such as flowers, fruit, ice, salt and grass to create ephemeral works of art that grow and decay. This experimental and transient quality enhances their beauty. Gallaccio's earlier works were frequently displayed in large derelict spaces, playing off their evocative context. In 1996 Gallaccio displayed a vast block of ice in a disused pumping station in East London. Over time, a core of rock salt slowly eroded the ice from the inside out. Though Gallaccio's work primarily engages the viewer visually, her work also captivates other senses with sound, scent and touch. Since there is often no physical evidence left from the installations, memory and ephemerality become emphasised when considering Gallaccio's work. Gallaccio's *Dirt Drawings* were created from natural materials sourced and collected whilst on a trip through Death Valley, the Grand Canyon and Arizona. Using traditional marbling techniques with organic materials Gallaccio subverted the traditional process to create something spontaneous and unpredictable.'
Thomas Dane Gallery

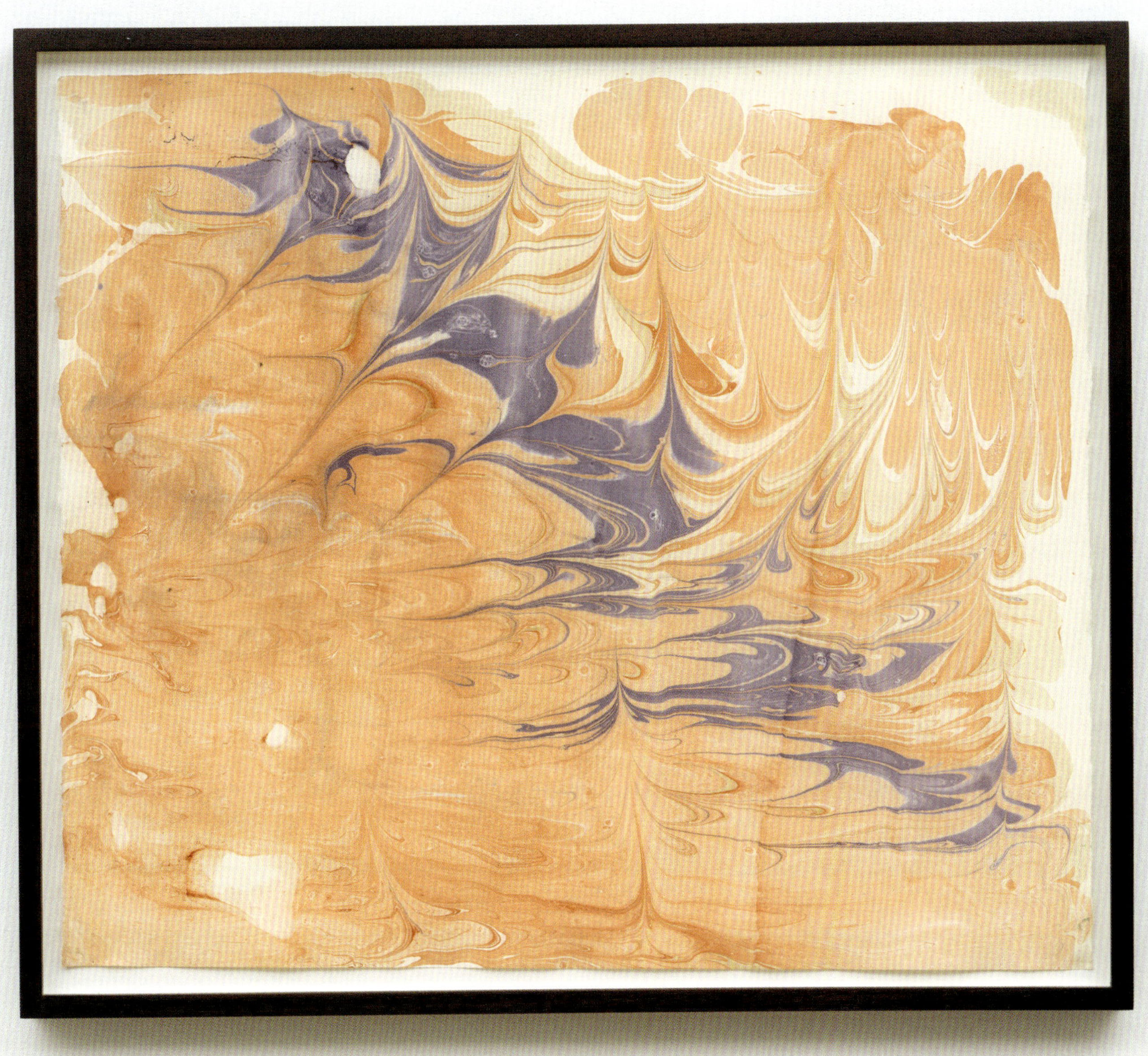

Andrew Hardwick RWA
Avonmouth, Saltings and Brown Estuary

2011 • oil, acrylic, emulsion, PVA, plaster, earth pigment, plastic, hay, ashes and other collage material on panel • 59 x 76 cm
courtesy the artist

I have always had an interest in earth. I remember, as a child, noticing how it coloured the wool of my family's sheep.

Also how this same earth then helped to colour the nearby Severn Estuary.

A few miles south, the soil changed from grey clay to bright red. So bright my Great Aunt had a disused redding mine in the field behind her house. I looked into the mine, very unsafe, dug directly and straight into the hill, I was told very firmly never to go in.

Redding was an earth used to make basic paint, often to mark sheep.

Older, helping on archaeological digs, I was fascinated how archaeologists could read the past by looking at subtle layers, colours and stains in the earths.

As a painter, in a similar vein, I began collecting earths to use in my work. I revisit land near my Great Aunt's for the very red soils; I also get local browns, blacks and colours from Cornwall. I enjoy how, mixed, or in their natural state, they create a rawness not obtainable with commercial oil paint.

In my work, I like to contrast wilderness with development and suggest memories, histories that still exist in the layers of the landscape.

Earth, rock, vegetation alongside tarmac and cement all helped along the way with oil paint, plastics from factories and chemical works.

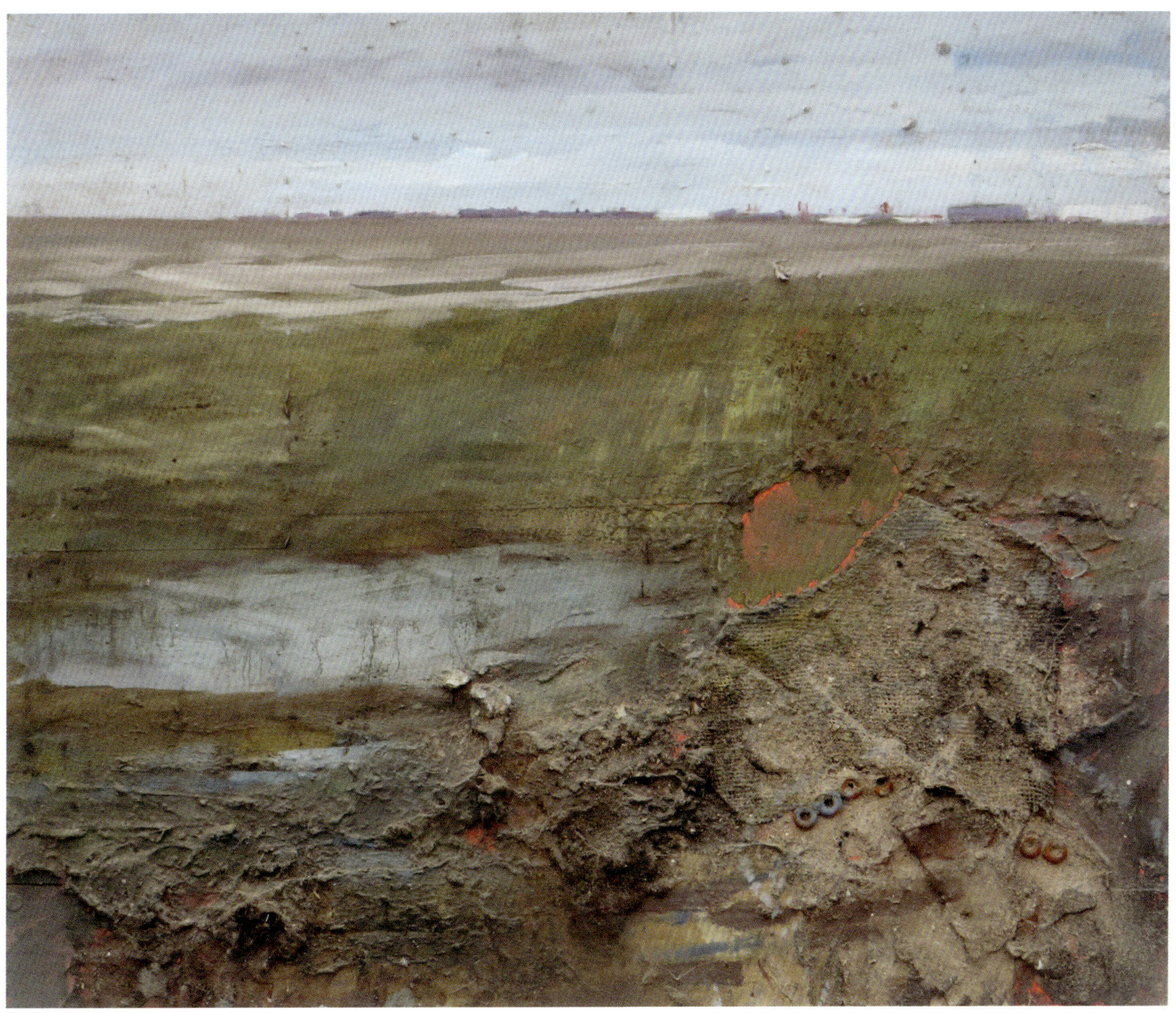

Rodney Harris MRSS

‘A Delineation of the Strata of England and Wales, with part of Scotland, Ireland, France’

2015 • print, 15 sections, ground rock on Somerset paper • 250 x 170 cm
courtesy the artist and School of Earth Sciences Collection, University of Bristol

During my Leverhulme Residency at Bristol University’s Earth Sciences department in 2015 I made *‘A Delineation of Strata …’*, a large-scale print, based on the first geological map of Britain by William Smith in 1815. It is made to the exact scale of Smith’s original map of fifteen prints.

Smith’s map identified where specific minerals could be found, enabling others to capitalise on this new knowledge. Whilst Smith distinguished different rock types using coloured inks available at the time, I made my inks by grinding down samples of rock collected from the different geological areas shown on the print. This ground rock was then mixed with oil to reveal the actual colour of the ground beneath our feet.

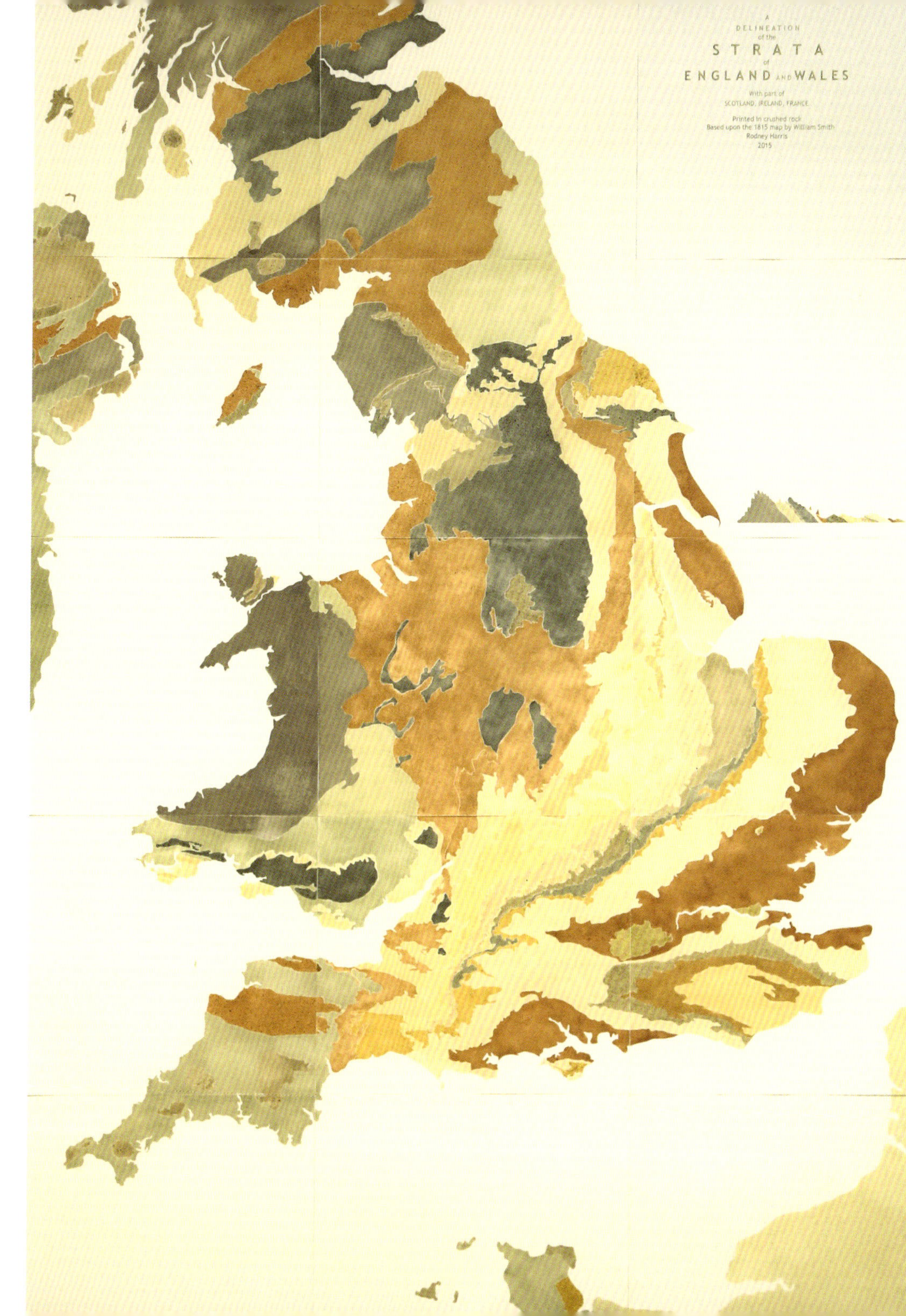
A
DELINEATION
of the
STRATA
of
ENGLAND AND WALES
With part of
SCOTLAND, IRELAND, FRANCE
Printed in crushed rock
Based upon the 1815 map by William Smith
Rodney Harris
2015

Fiona Hingston
Field Walking No.1

2007 · earth and ink on paper · 125 x 125 cm
courtesy the artist

A ploughed field was a signifier of changing seasons, a rotation of pasture land for the herd or the sowing of maize and other crops. As I walked these fields, along deep furrows – I was held, grounded in weight and wetness, the smell of minerals released by the plough filling the air. One particular area smelt of blood.

Fifteen years on from the making of these drawings there are no cows, no crops, no ploughing, no muck. Farm buildings are dilapidated, earmarked for housing. Fields are now harrowed, pumped with nitrogen, sown with grass that never seeds, and contractors on huge machinery cut silage three times a year.

A mono culture.

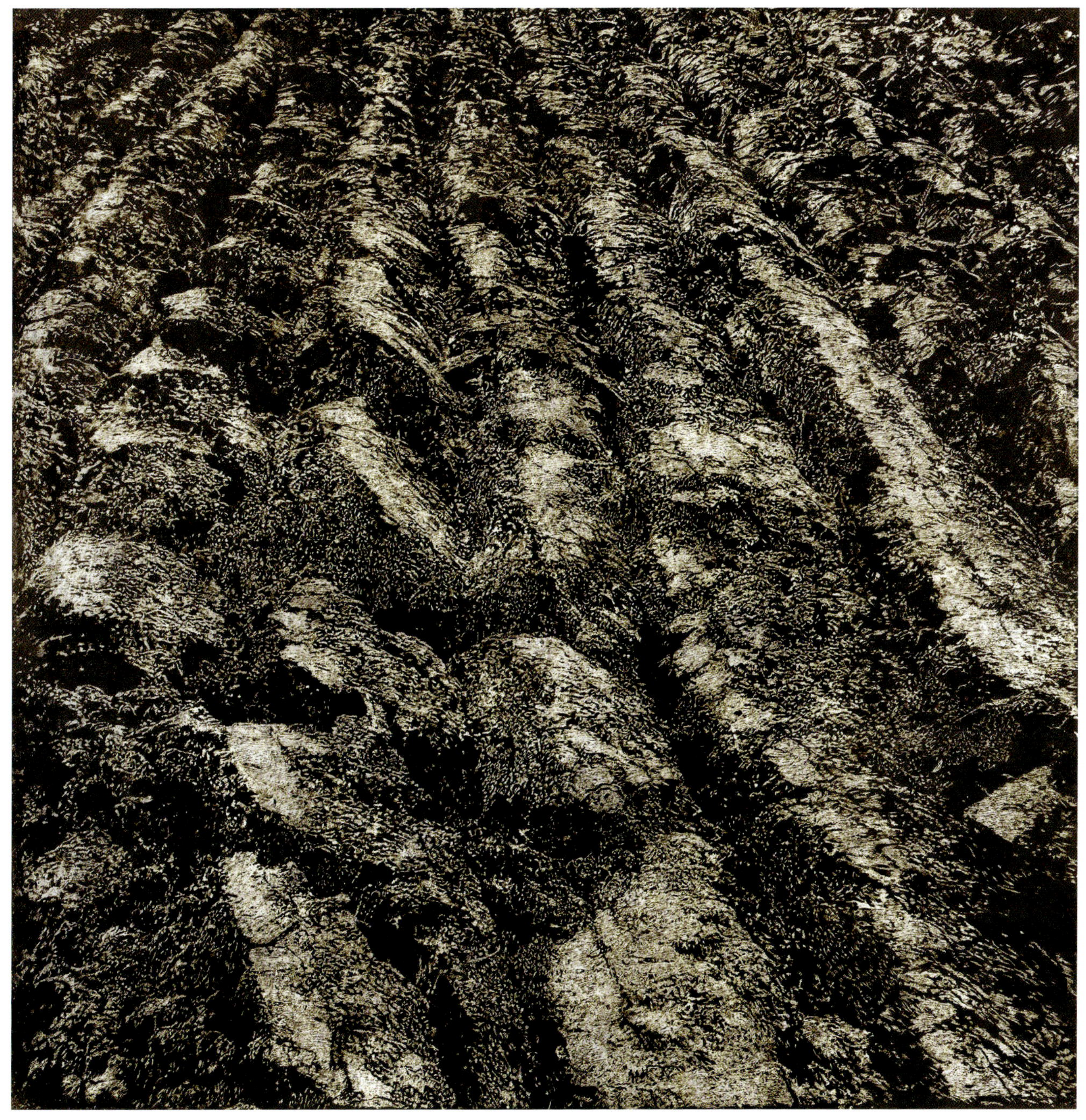

Kabir Hussain
Stone 2

2017 • bronze • 9 x 9 x 7 cm
courtesy the artist • photograph Jonathan Callery

From 2016 to 2017 I watched Field TM 3562 2815. My preconceptions of a formal study of landscape were unsettled as the soil changed from blacks to browns, specks joined to present a sea of green as the seedlings started to lift the field. Initially everything felt pastoral, I sensed a presence. In autumn the leaves shrank, disturbingly the life-force was being drawn into the soil. In violent eruptions, intoxicated by a sugar rush, the multi-limbed giant beasts forced themselves into the world; during the cold winter sugar beet 'Campaign' the harvesters lifted them with beet hooks, holding them by the roots, and swiftly, with a single stroke, decapitated.

In the field stones lay silently, they stoically observed the activity around them, like tubers they became an equivalent crop. I took inspiration from the Renaissance painting tradition of translating stones into mountains. Manipulating wax I grafted my excursions into the topography of the field directly upon the body of the stone. They became a hybrid, an artefact-essay.

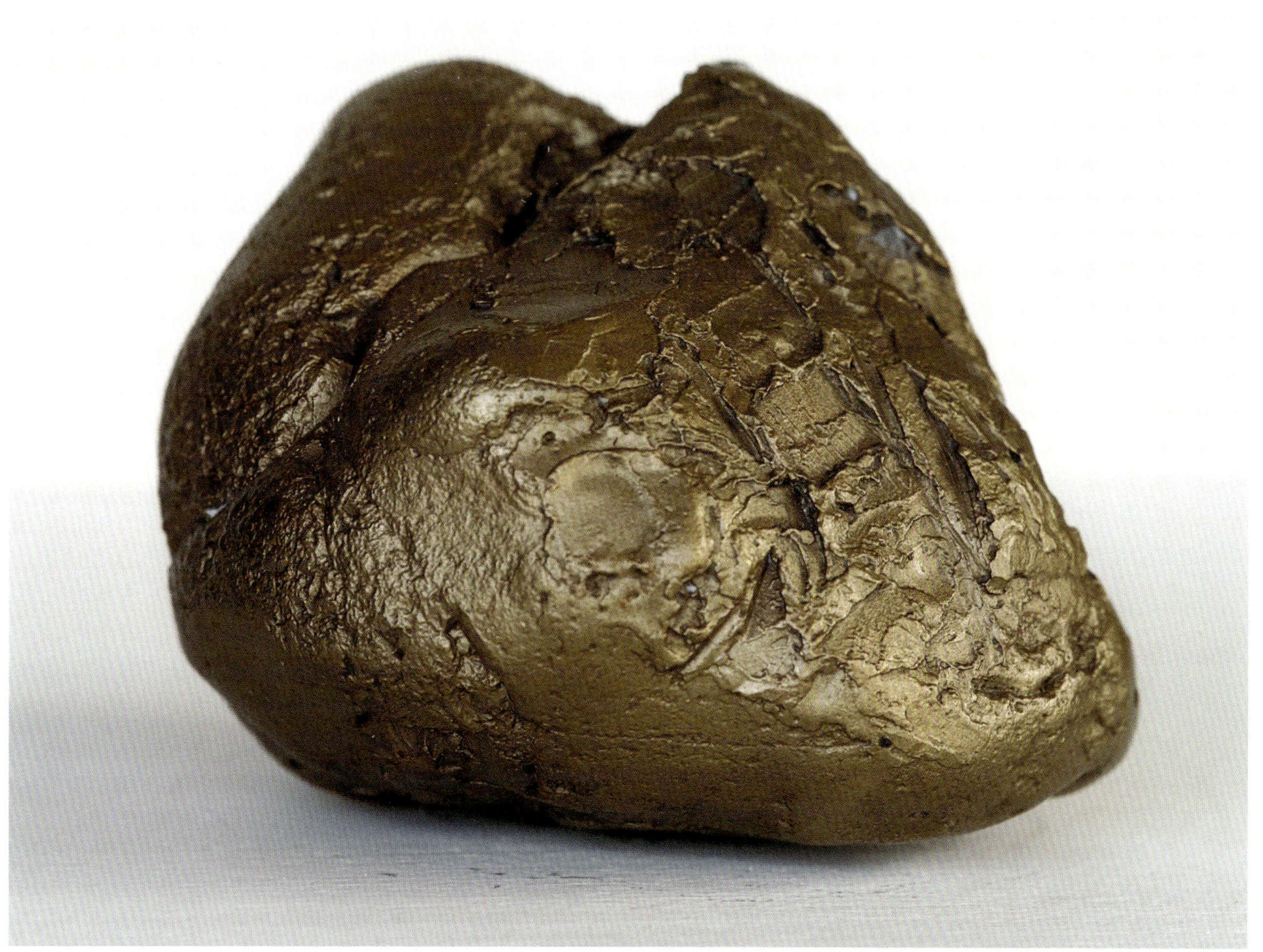

Tania Kovats
Strike

2001 • mixed-media sculpture, acrylic composite and MDF • 109 x 162 x 85 cm
Towner Eastbourne

'*Strike* takes the form of a white plinth eroded into a rocky, weather-beaten landscape. Its scale is minimised yet it maintains a monumental presence in the centre of the gallery space. The sculpture is reminiscent of a jagged and dangerous cliff face, such as that of Beachy Head and the cliffs of the Seven Sisters. It acknowledges the unseen and intangible forces of nature that give 'an edge' to the landscape.

'In her work Kovats deals with the experience and understanding of landscape. She frequently takes a geological approach, investigating the effects of subterranean shifts on the rocks that are seen on the surface. She looks at natural disasters within the landscape, at the patterns of fault lines and the scars they carve across countries and continents.'
Towner Eastbourne

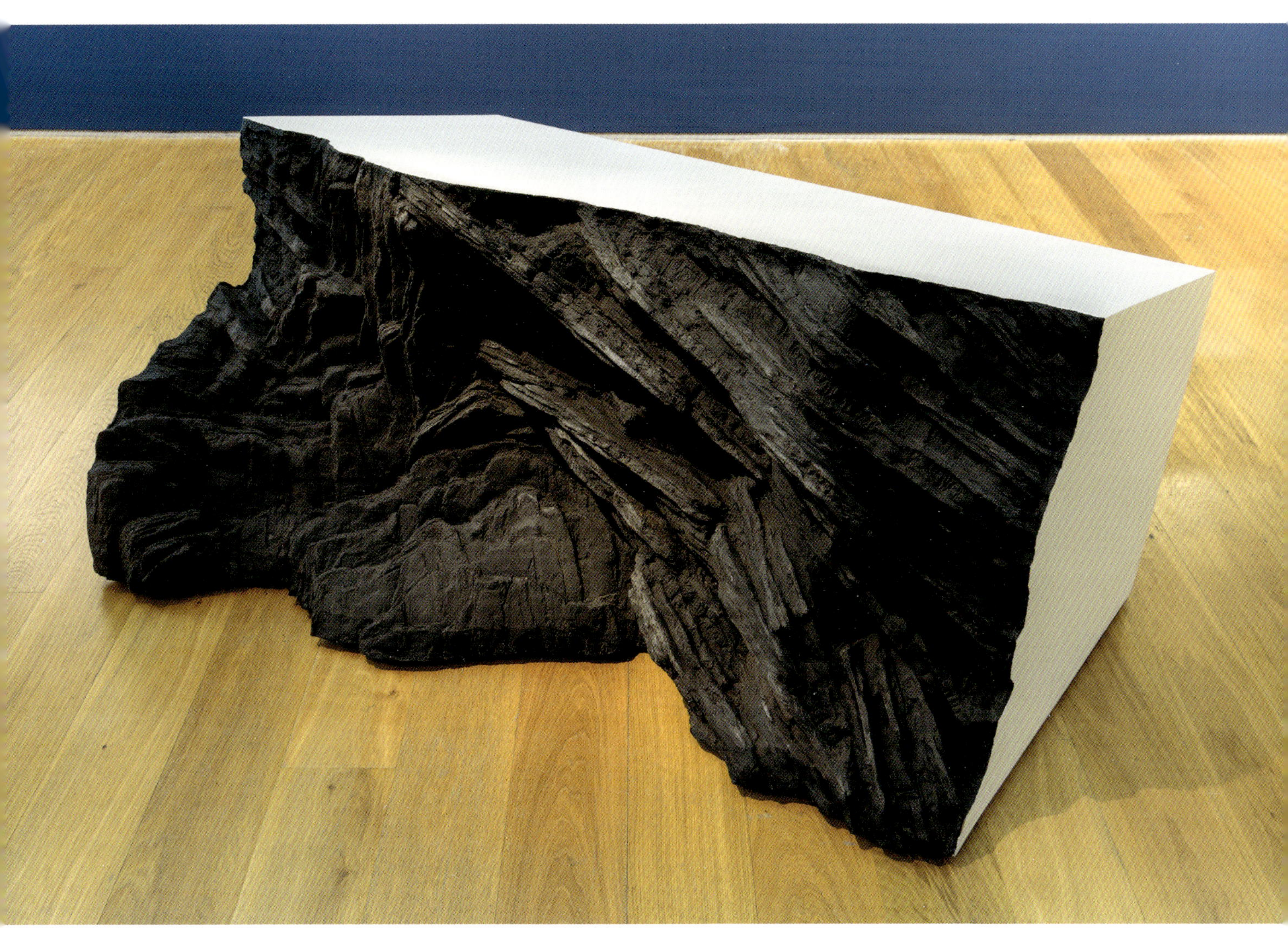

Abigail Lane
Molehills

2016 • painted bronze • 38 x 33 x 14 cm and 23.5 x 20 x 7.5 cm
courtesy the artist and Agnés Rein

'True, without falsehood, certain and most true, that which is above is the same as that which is below, and that which is below is the same as that which is above, for the performance of miracles of the one thing. And as all things are from the one, by the meditation of one, so all things have their birth from this one thing by adaptation. The Sun is its Father, the Moon its Mother, the Wind carries it in its belly, and its nurse is the Earth. This is the Father of all perfection, or consummation of the whole world. Its power is integrating, if it be turned into earth.'

The above passage , one of several similar translations, originates from the Hermetic texts. The transcription, originating from the Middle Ages and said to have been inscribed into a now lost green crystal slab known as the Emerald Tablet, was, according to legend, discovered in a caved tomb clutched in the hands of its corpse-author, Hermes Trismegistus. The text expresses ideas that connect the microcosm with the macrocosm: the belief that smaller systems are miniature versions of the larger universe, that each will inform the other and that the powers of the cosmic soul must be concentrated into solid material. Galaxy and atom, mind and body, sensation and its stimulant are intimately bound – and we are stardust as it turns out.

Its origins, history and translations are somewhat dubious – repeatedly mythologised and speculated upon. However, it is the debate and the somewhat magical musing that interests rather than the truth. Through science we forever strive to illuminate and reach certainties that explain the mysteries of life, planets, their forces, laws and origin, while somewhat schizophrenically we cherish and indulge in the wonder of the mystifying, unknown or yet to be understood.

Mystery is a seductive and powerful force. Humans love the striptease of discovery with the storytelling that develops hand in hand and yet in our lived lives we are impatient. We are restless in the knowledge that we each have only the time that is ours – and that itches. It is our ongoing nature to scratch the surface, scrape and pick to get through ... to the above and the below, to get in and to get out in every which way to address the persistent itching.

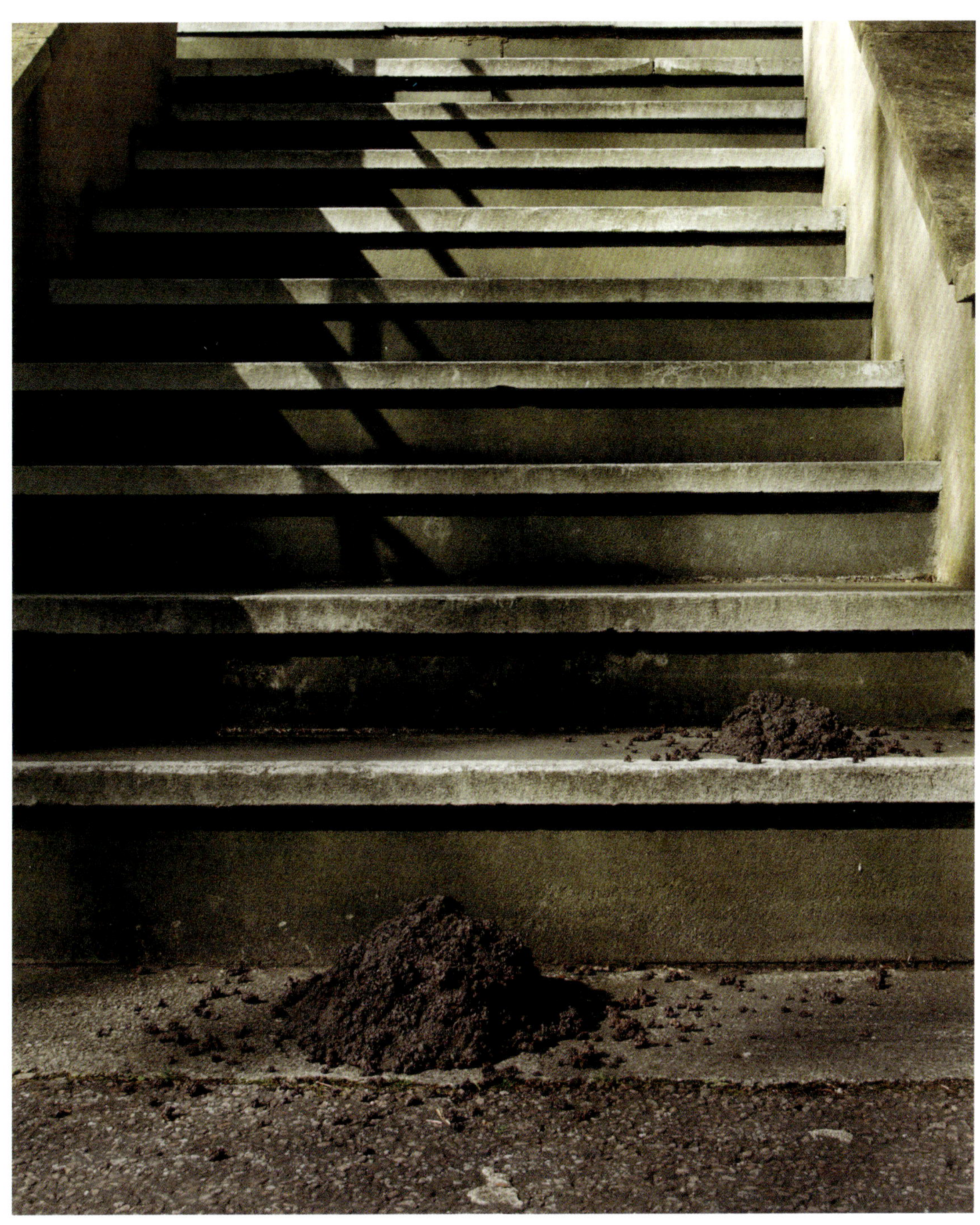

Richard Long CBE RA RWA

RAILWAY LINE
A PAIR OF BUZZARDS
THISTLES
IRISHMAN'S WALL
WHITEHORSE HILL
STATTS HOUSE
WINNEY'S DOWN
EAST DART RIVER
SANDY HOLE PASS
A DEAD SHEEP
BROAD DOWN
SHEEP BONES
COTTON GRASS
CLAPPER BRIDGE
MIDDAY
GORSE
GRANITE BOULDERS
SECOND FOX
SMALL WOOD
WEST DART RIVER
NAKER'S HILL
FOX
OLD CHINA CLAY WORKINGS
RED LAKE
PONIES
FIRST SUN
CAIRN
BRACKEN
STONE ROW

A STRAIGHT NORTHWARD WALK ACROSS DARTMOOR

1979

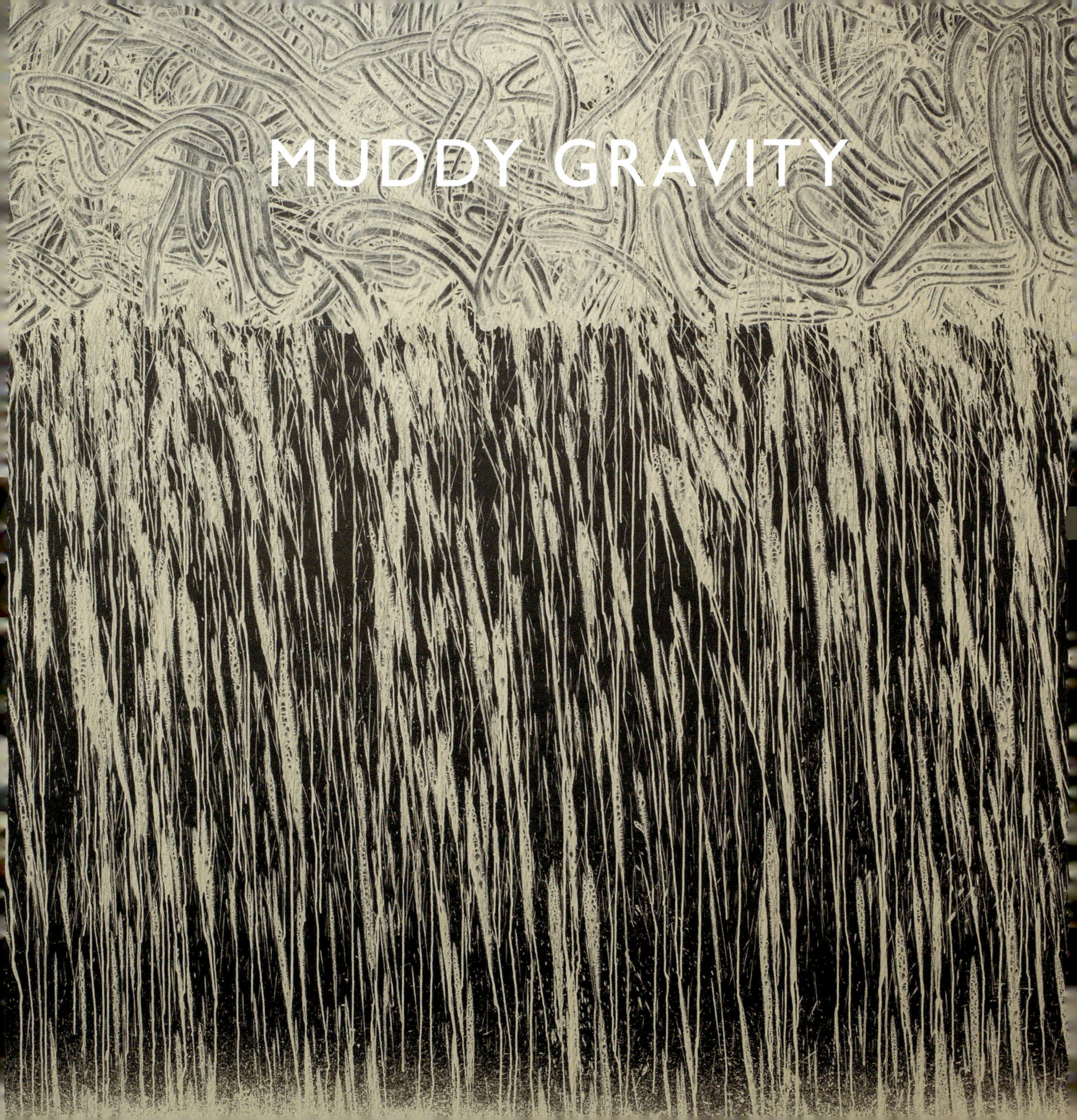
MUDDY GRAVITY

Siobhán McDonald
A History of Time

2018 • photogenic drawings: silver nitrate, light and our earliest plants on antique paper • 43 x 52 cm
courtesy the artist

A History of Time are photogenic drawings that narrate the changing state of the Earth's atmosphere. To make this work the light has travelled through atmospheres with varying levels of carbon dioxide, recreating the conditions of the Triassic, Cretaceous, and Devonian Periods and the Anthropocene Epoch respectively. The light has been blocked by fossil leaves foraged from our earliest plants on earth.

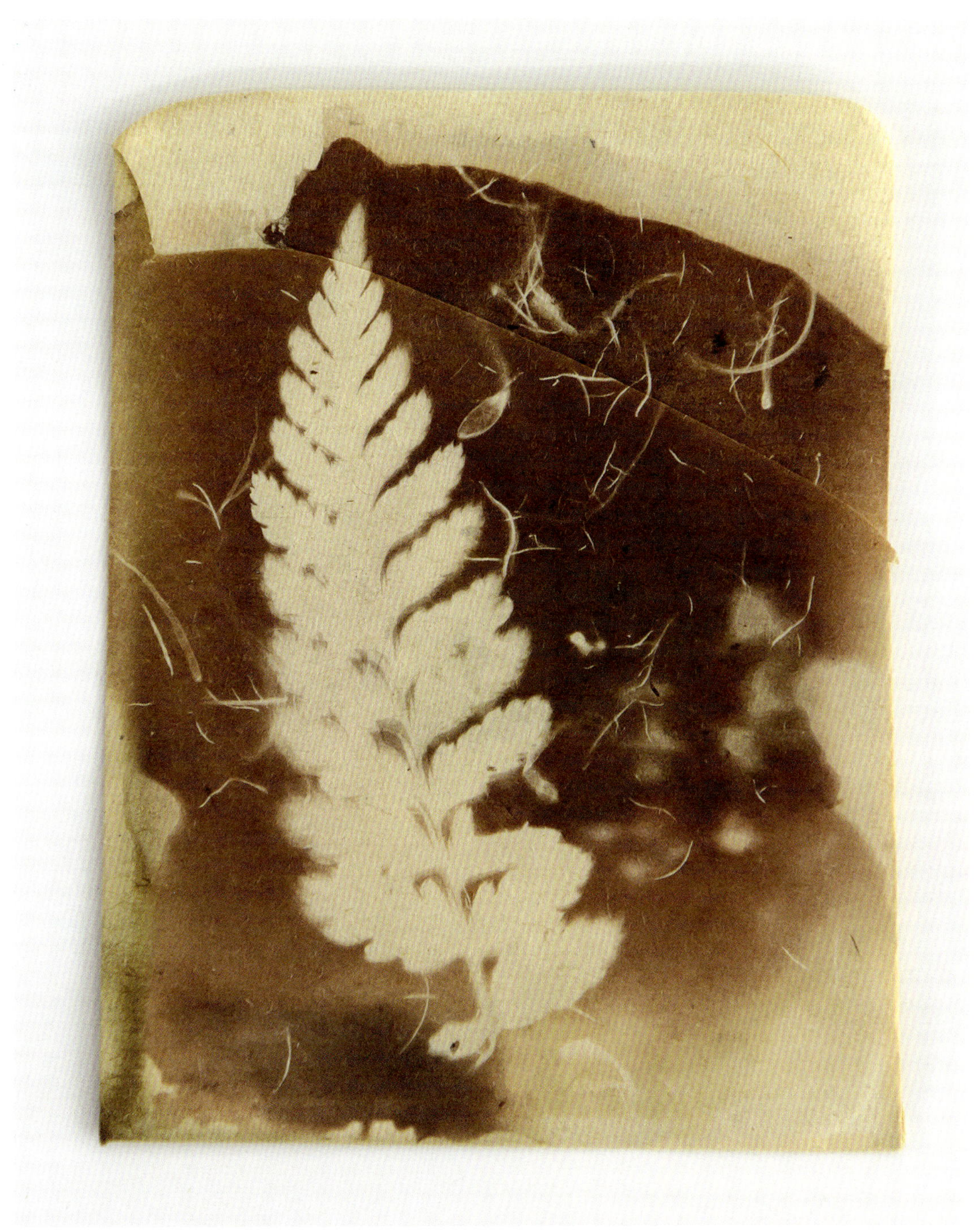

David Nash OBE RA
Wooden Boulder

1978 • oak sphere being cut out of the trunk, the start of the boulder's journey
courtesy the artist • image David Nash

Wooden Boulder.

The safest way to move the wooden boulder from the fallen oak where it was carved to my studio was by levering it down a stream. In 1978 the boulder jammed itself into a waterfall and so began its new life as a free-range sculpture, moved downstream by a succession of storm water and later in the Dwyryd Estuary, by tides. It was last seen August 2015.

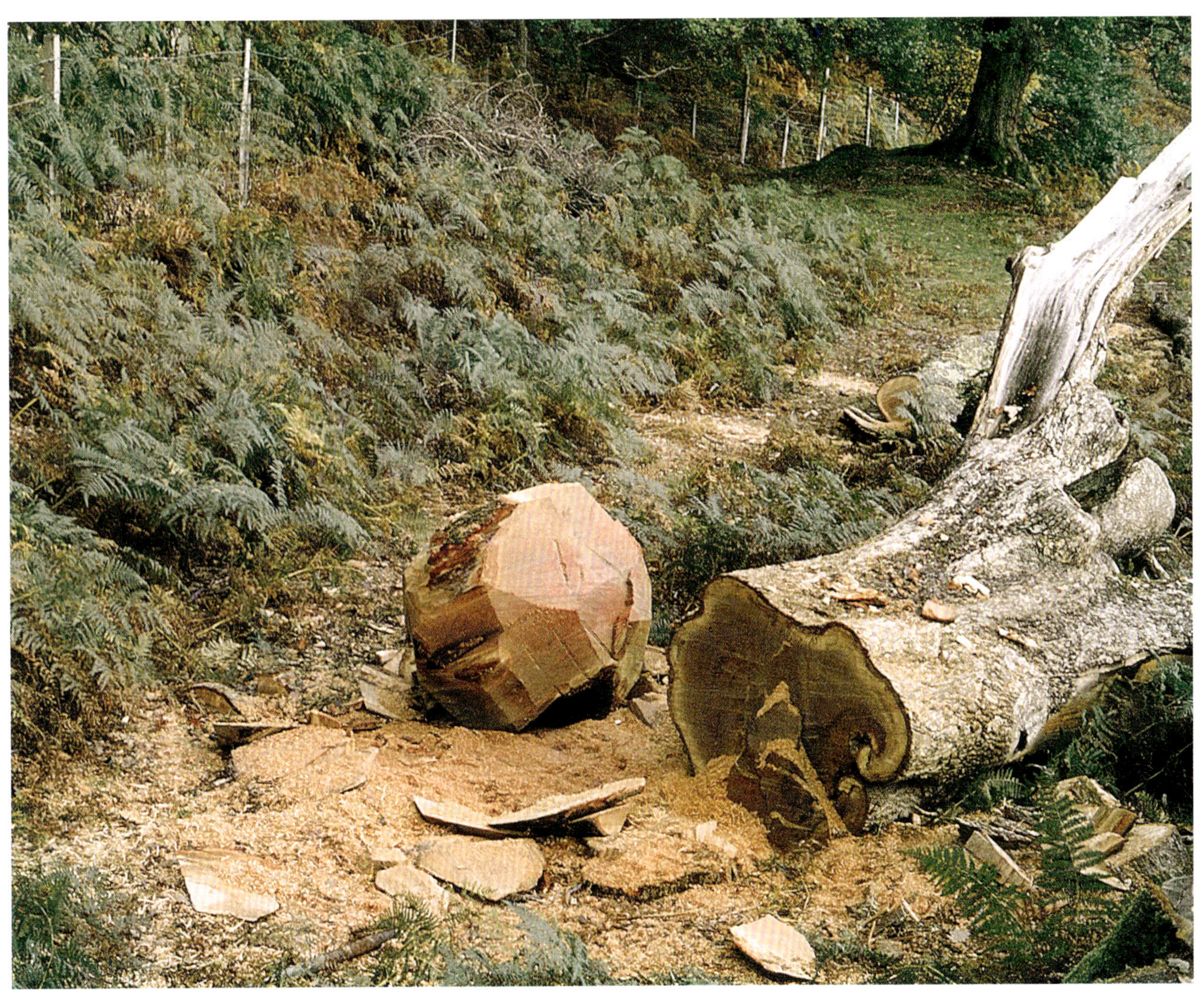

Mariele Neudecker
Everything and Nothing

2007 • MDF, paper, wood, plasticine, jesmonite, acrylic paint • 29 x 35 x 152 cm
courtesy the artist • © Mariele Neudecker • photograph Benjamin Jones

We were not there, when the water was, ... or the tectonic forces were so very powerful, microorganisms too tiny for humans to see, the pressure imperceivable, and the atmospheric influences invisible ... to create such cavernous spaces.

And ... my knowledge of these 'holes in the ground' is rather limited. I was never into caving. But still. The images always struck me, a path, disappearing in the dark.

Human perception is limited as it is – and the image of a cave opening brings about notions of 'big time' and re-percussions of eye-sockets, ear-canals, bodily cavities and crevices. However: ... there are materialities and realities at play here that entice the viewer to imagine space, to propose different scales and connect a mixture of gaps into a different 'understanding' of two or more realities at once – it is mysterious, unassuming and familiar, all at the same time.

The formation and development of caves can occur over the course of millions of years. This is 'hard to comprehend' – a very long time. The earliest human remaining communications in caves happened many thousands of years ago – which is slightly easier to take in.

How little it takes, to transport the human mind into other worlds and layers of reality? Not much, ... and right in front of you: a wooden box, some plasticine and a model of a disappearing cave ... that mean *everything* and *nothing*, ... it allows the imagination to open up endless possibilities.

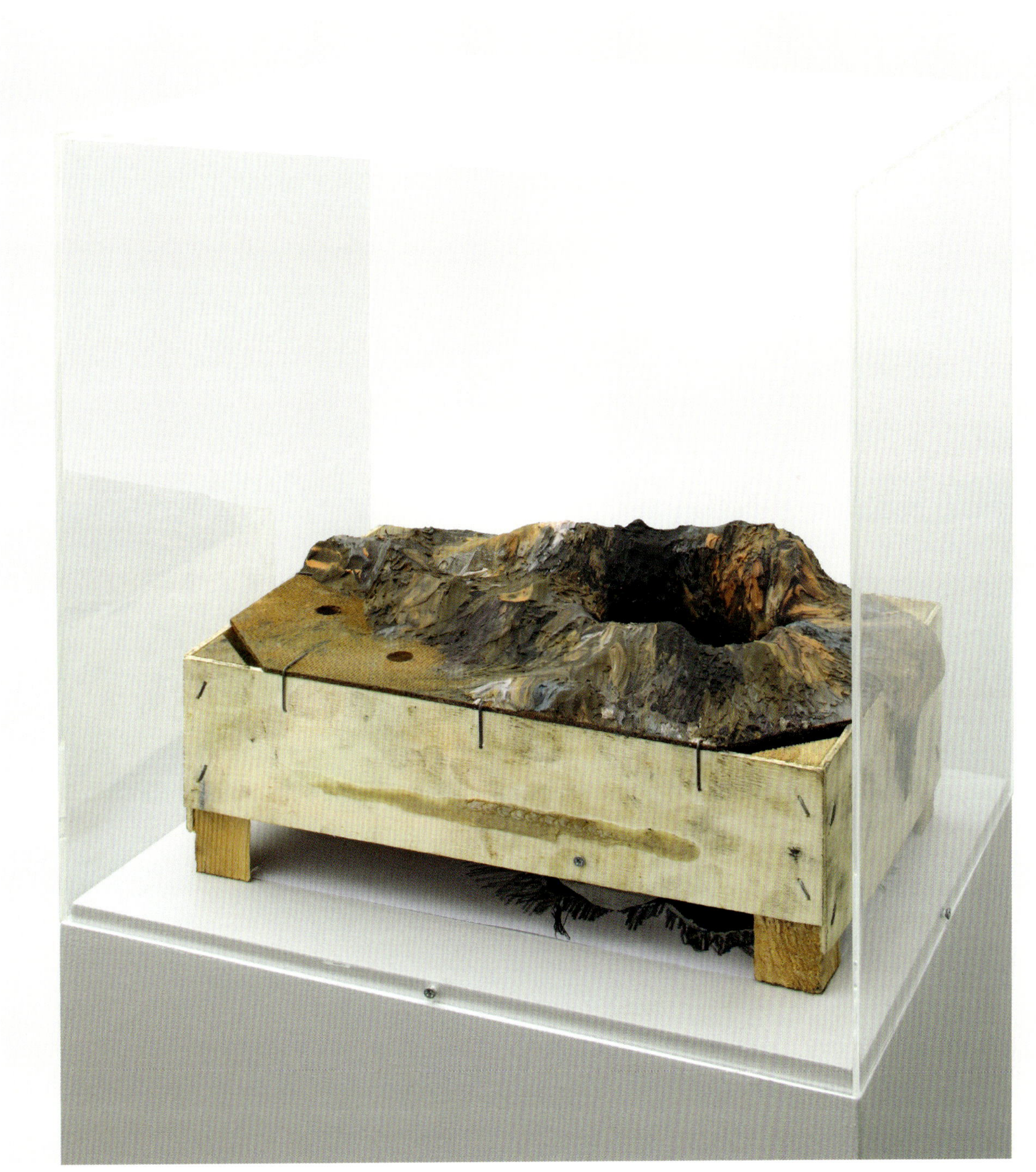

Katie Paterson
Fossil Necklace

2013 • hand-carved fossil beads x 170 • 147.3 x 73.7 cm
private collection • courtesy the artist and Ingleby Gallery
photograph © MJC (exhibition view Kettle's Yard)

Fossil Necklace is a string of worlds; comprised of 170 carved, rounded beads, with each bead modestly representing a major event in the evolution of life through a vast expanse of geological time. From the mono-cellular origins of life to the shifting of the continents, the extinction of the Cretaceous period triggered by a falling meteorite, to the first flowering of flowers, it charts the development of our species and affirms our intimate connection to the evolution of those alongside us. Each fossil has been individually selected from all corners of the globe, and then carved into spherical beads in a secondary process of excavation.

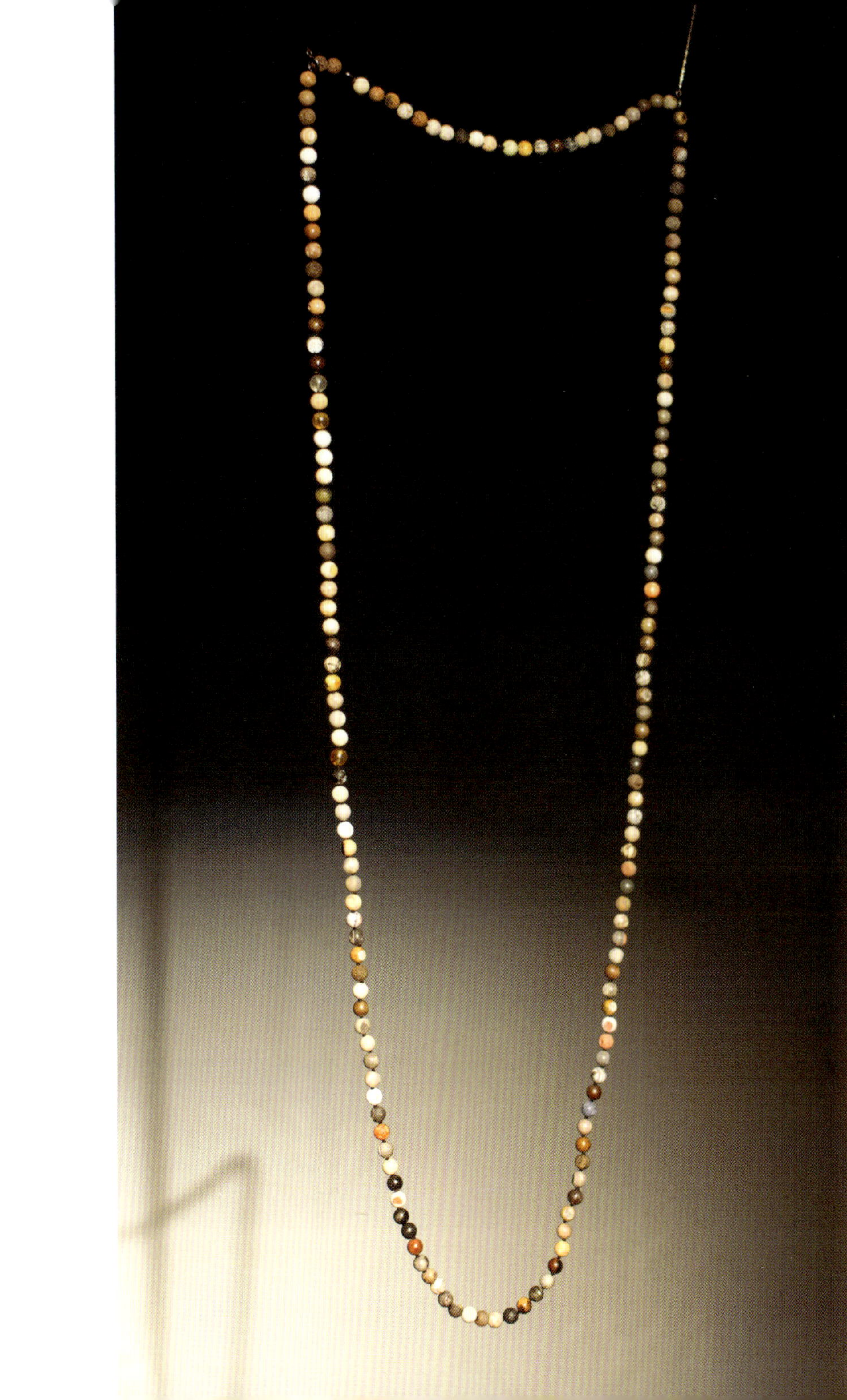

Julian Perry
Fanfare 34

2010 • oil on panel • 103.5 x 122 cm
courtesy the artist

A terrible thing.

It is a terrible thing but in the twelve years since I painted *Fanfare 34* the CO_2 in the atmosphere has risen by 8%. The work was the lead image in my London show 'An Extraordinary Prospect'. An exhibition with the simple aim of using coastal erosion to represent a world under threat from Climate Change.

There has always been erosion but even back in 2010 it was obvious that sea levels were rising, and rates of land lost were increasing.

My work has always been committed to examining mankind's uneasy relationship with the natural world. A relationship that is flawed and dysfunctional but therefore rich in potential subjects. I hope my paintings are poignant and emblematic, reflecting the state of our landscape both good and bad. Brownfield sites, nature reserves, caravan parks and doomed allotment sheds have all been subjects for past shows. Recent works have looked at the crisis in British forests due to disease and stress exacerbated by climate breakdown and airborne pollutants. Coastal erosion is, however, my ongoing fascination and the subject of my recent show in Southampton.

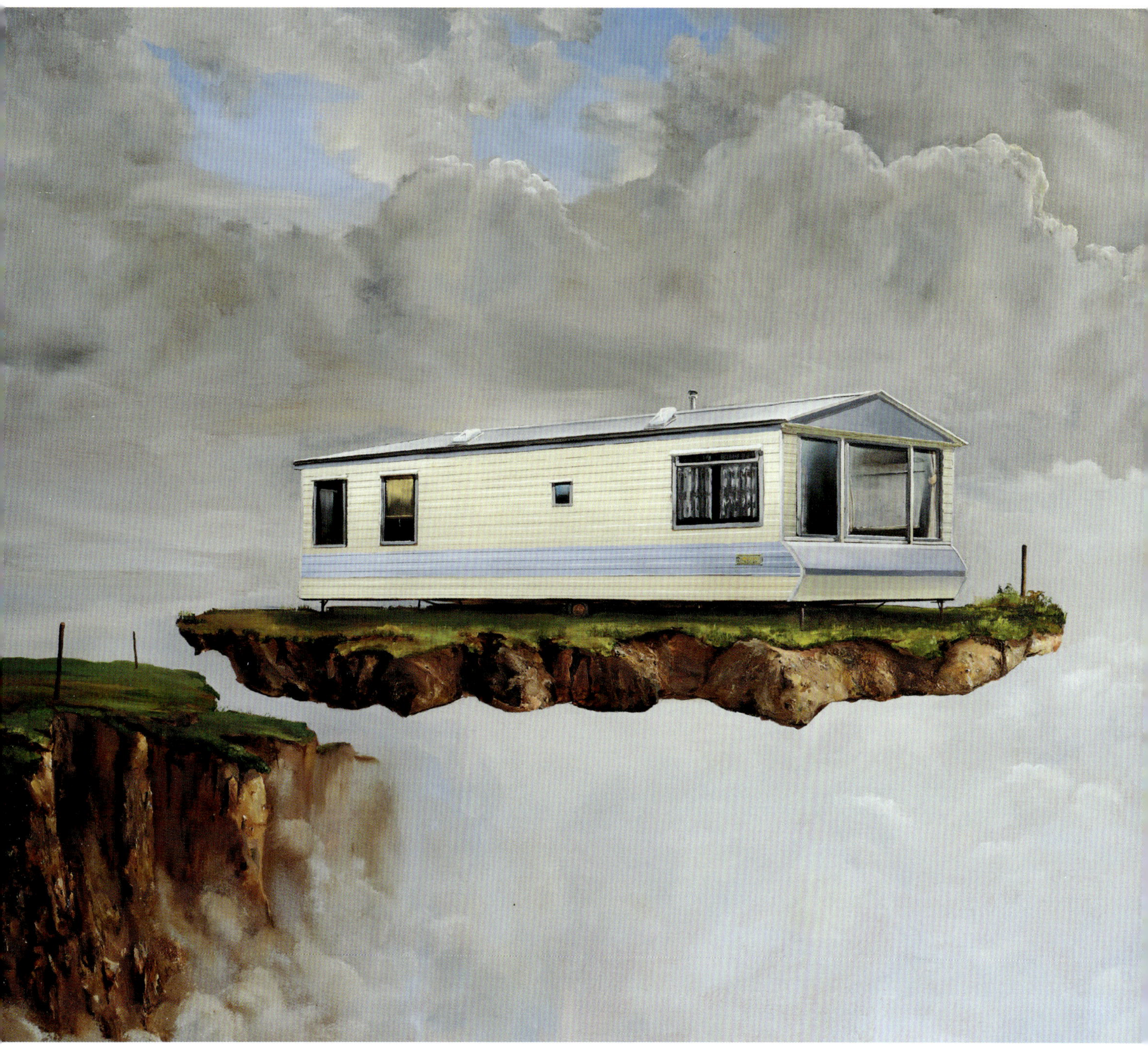

Michael Porter RWA
Dirt series 12-07-21

2021 • gouache on heritage paper • 45 x 32 cm
courtesy the artist • © M. Porter

She was digging the earth, separating the weeds and tendrils, throwing them to one side before dividing the organic matter from the clinging dirt.

The garden was full of flowers in various stages of bloom; glancing at these tangled clumps beside these much brighter coloured cultivated flowers highlighted their differences, both in the way I perceived them and their physical appearance.

In order to experience heat we also have to understand what it is to be cold; to recognise beauty we must have something to measure it against, if not ugliness then something which questions our notion of the beautiful.

We are brought up to accept what constitutes the picturesque, until it gets assimilated into our way of looking at the world. Everyone has a unique way of interpreting the world around us, unfortunately this uniqueness is often suppressed through conformity and acceptance.

A small clump of tangled earth, 'Dirt', something which is usually overlooked, discarded and thrown to one side, is worth the second glance and maybe even more than a second glance.

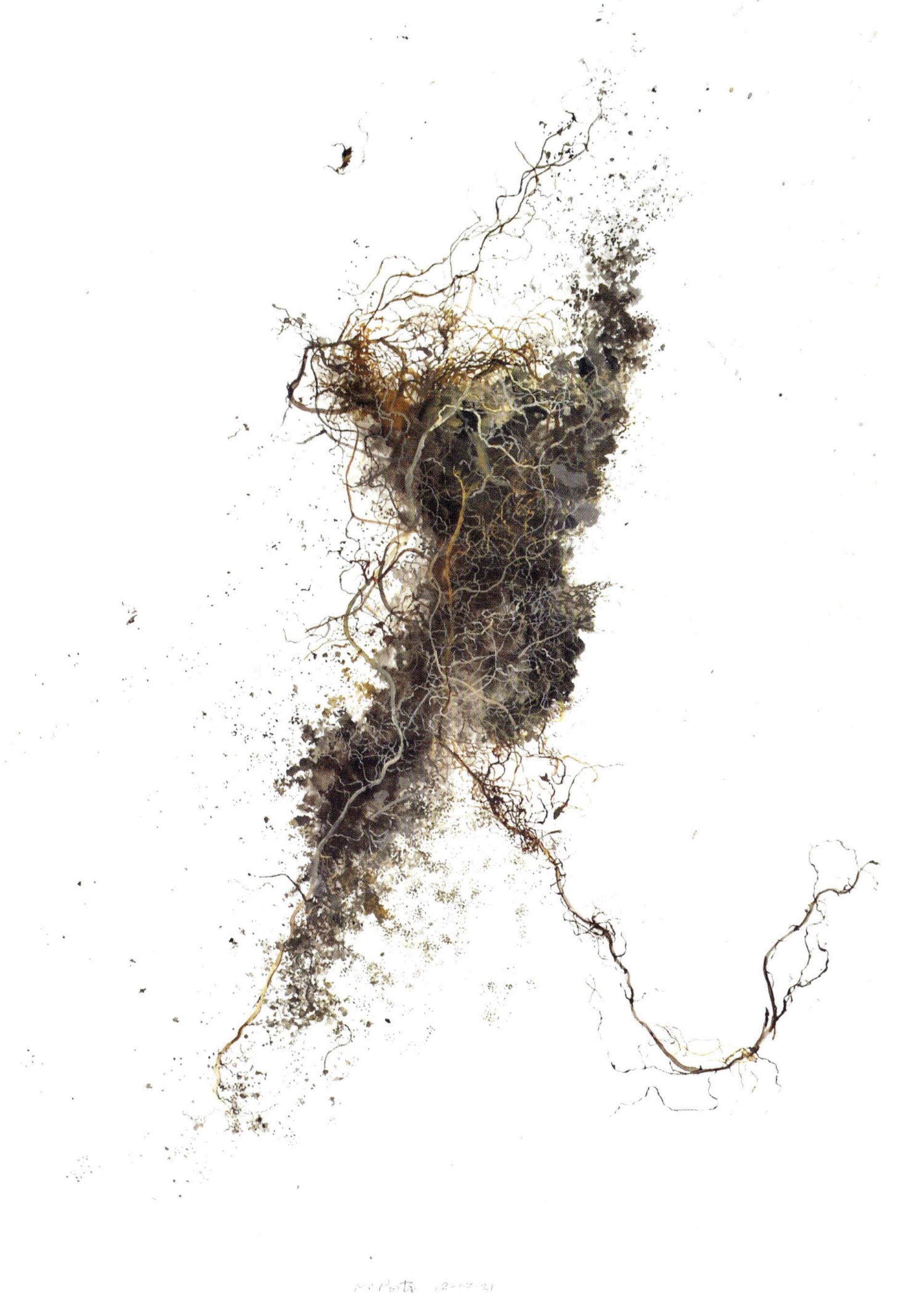

Kathy Prendergast
Chimborazo

2010 • ink and gouache on printed map • 65 x 52 cm
courtesy the artist • image: Kathy Prendergast

Chimborazo, the furthest place from the centre of the earth, digs deepest.

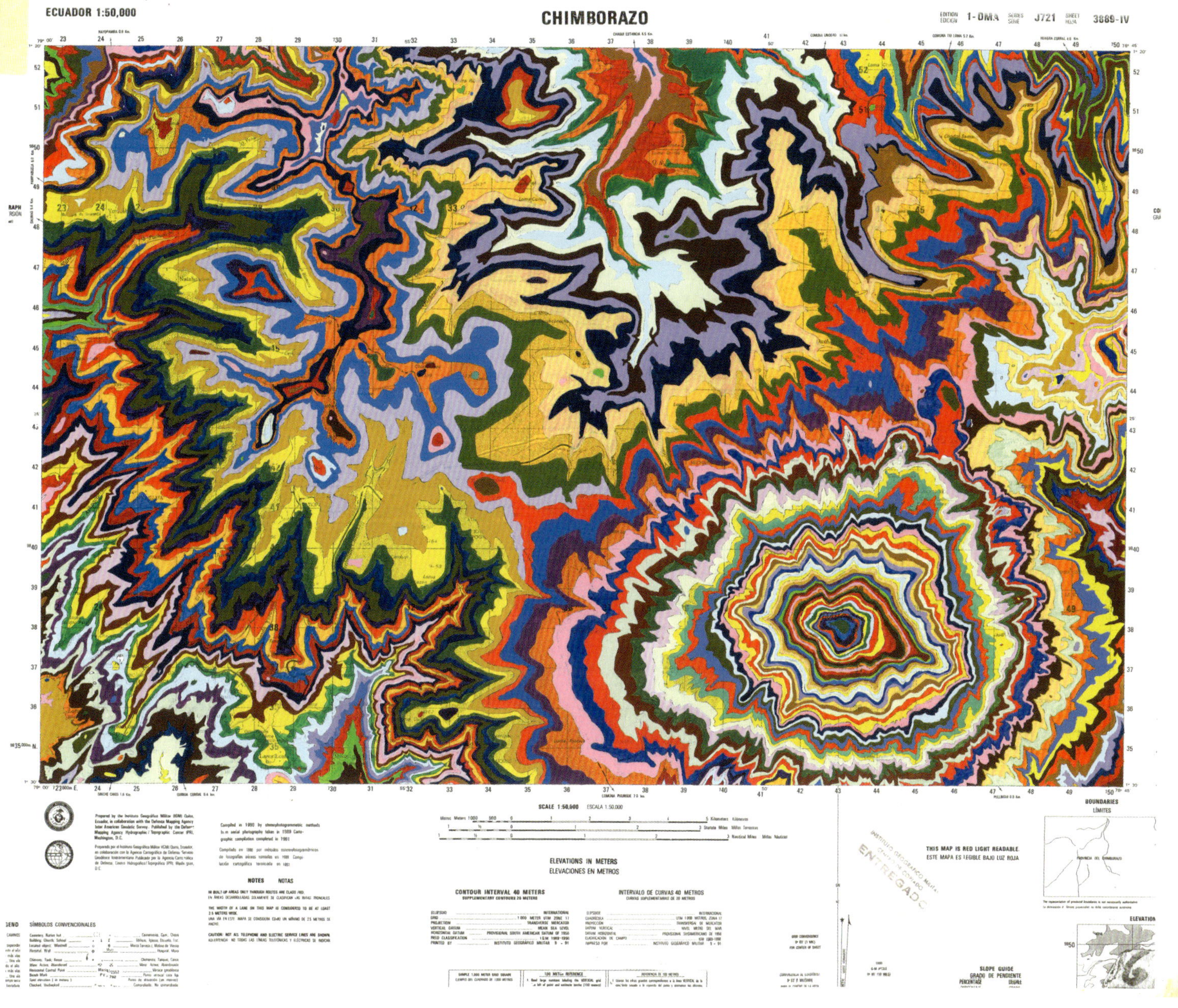
ECUADOR 1:50,000
CHIMBORAZO
EDITION 1-DMA
SERIES J721
SHEET 3889-IV
SCALE 1:50,000 ESCALA 1:50.000
ELEVATIONS IN METERS
ELEVACIONES EN METROS
NOTES NOTAS
CONTOUR INTERVAL 40 METERS
INTERVALO DE CURVAS 40 METROS
THIS MAP IS RED LIGHT READABLE.
ESTE MAPA ES LEGIBLE BAJO LUZ ROJA
BOUNDARIES
LIMITES
SLOPE GUIDE
GRADO DE PENDIENTE
ENTREGADO

Carol Rhodes · 1959-2018
Factory Roof, Countryside

2002 · oil on board · 46.9 x 56.9 x 1.7 cm
Southampton City Art Gallery · © Carol Rhodes Estate
courtesy Alison Jacques, London

I have spoken before of how conscious I am of giving everything a sort of equal status in the pictures, which is enabled by the aerial view, seeing the landscape top to bottom, not near and far. Front doesn't have priority over middle-ground, middle-ground over background; it's sort of spatially egalitarian. Also being interested and excited by the backs of buildings and places, not the fronts. All these things may sound slight in themselves, or 'merely' formal, but they're all part of what makes a painting and gives it meaning and power.

from 'Carol Rhodes and Andrew Mummery in conversation' in *Carol Rhodes* (Milan: Skira editore, 2018)
© Carol Rhodes Estate

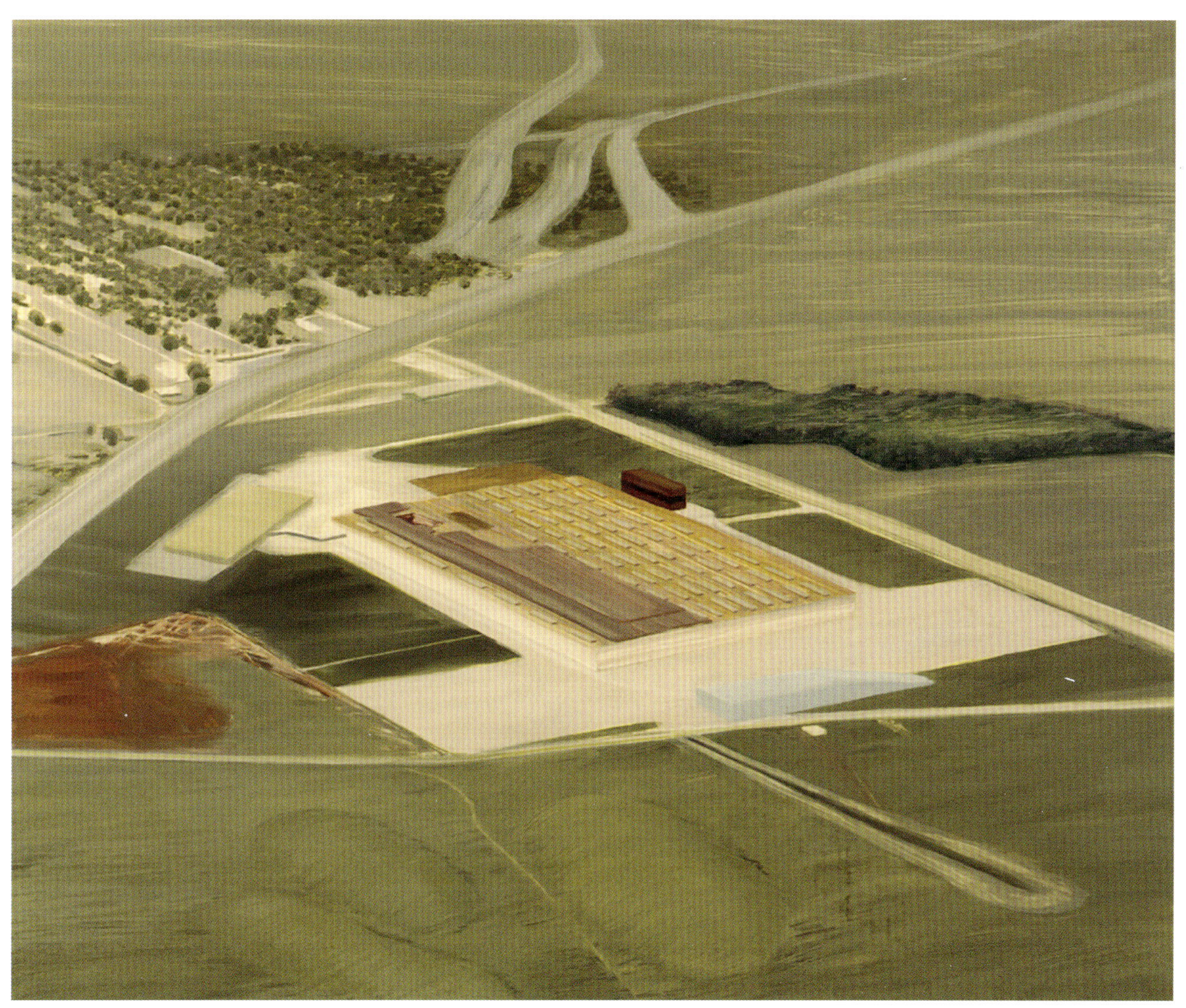

Yinka Shonibare CBE RA
Earth Kid (Boy)

2020 • fibreglass mannequin, Dutch wax printed cotton textile, globe, brass, steel baseplate, fishnet with plastics • 124 x 56 x 85 cm
courtesy the artist and James Cohan Gallery, New York
photograph Stephen White & Co.

Earth Kid (Boy) represents the next generation of young activists fighting for climate justice, whose actions have thrown the spotlight on the failings of previous generations of policy makers. *Earth Kid (Boy)* bends under the weight of the collected plastics he has gathered through scavenging, with the intention of recycling. The globe on his shoulders shows maps: areas of global warming on the planet. His costume is made from Dutch wax batik fabric, a signature motif in all of the artist's work – the batiks were Indonesian-influenced fabrics, mass produced by the Dutch and then sold to West African colonies, and now are synonymous with African identity. Shonibare uses it throughout his work as a metaphor for post-colonial identity.

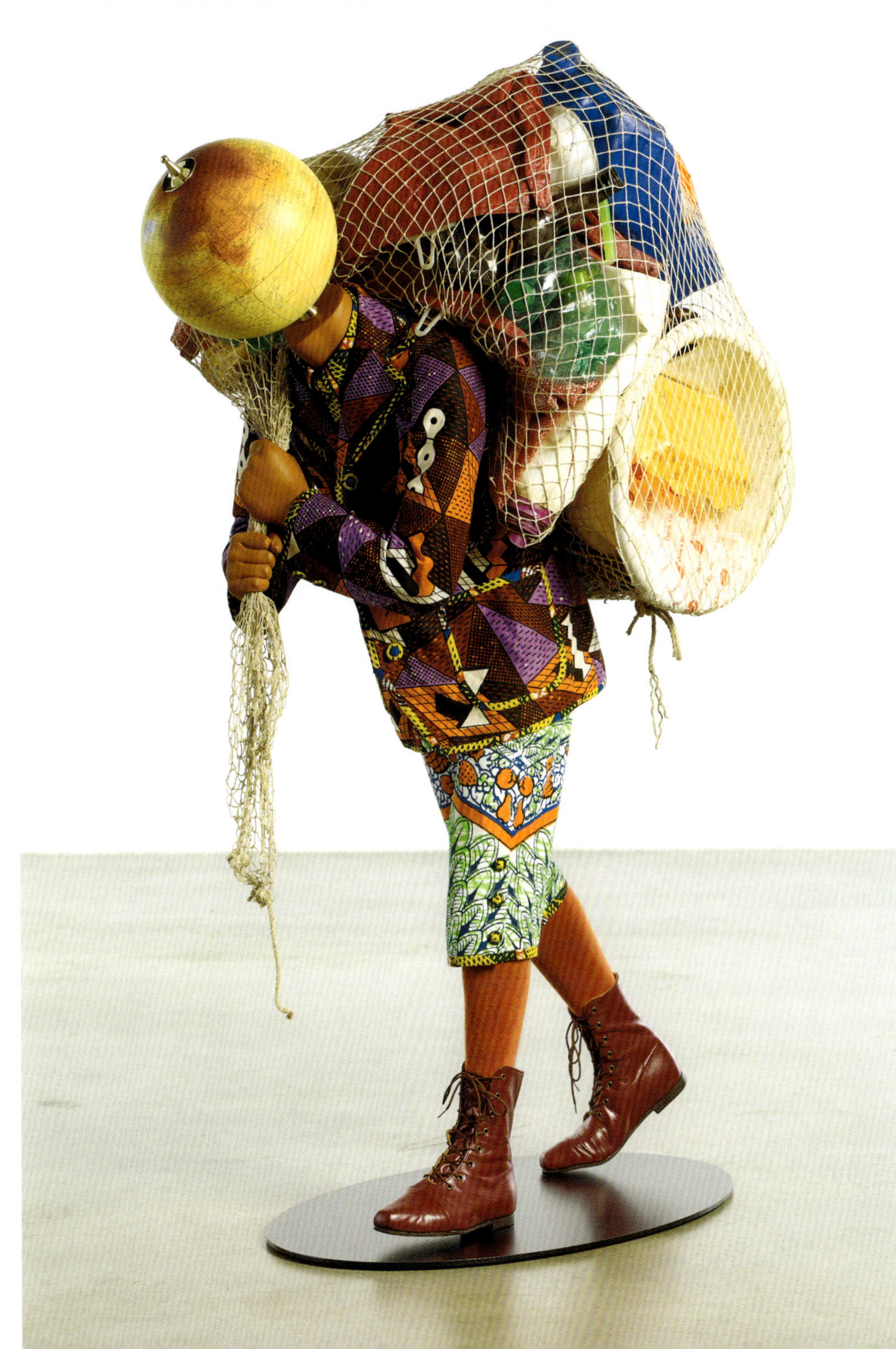

Emma Stibbon RA RWA
Broken Terrain

2017 • intaglio print: 2 plates • 67.5 x 80 cm
courtesy the artist

The uncertainty of solid ground fascinates me, the idea that a landscape is contingent and liable to transform is profound. I made *Broken Terrain* in response to a residency on Big Island, Hawai'i where I stayed on the rim of Kīlauea, one of the world's most active volcanoes. It depicts the broken lava pavement of Kīlauea Iki, a side eruption to the main volcano crater. Dramatic formations and breaks in the lava pavement are created when the upward pressure of the molten lava within a flow pushes or buckles the overlying crust. Walking on this unstable crater floor felt precarious and the ground was literally hot beneath my feet. Whilst out walking I gathered volcanic ash to incorporate with my drawing media to create a tactile surface in the print – I wanted to give a sense of the elemental terrain in the physical surface of the work. Volcanoes embody the primordial forces of nature that shape the Earth. A recurring theme in my work reflects on this tension between destruction and renewal.

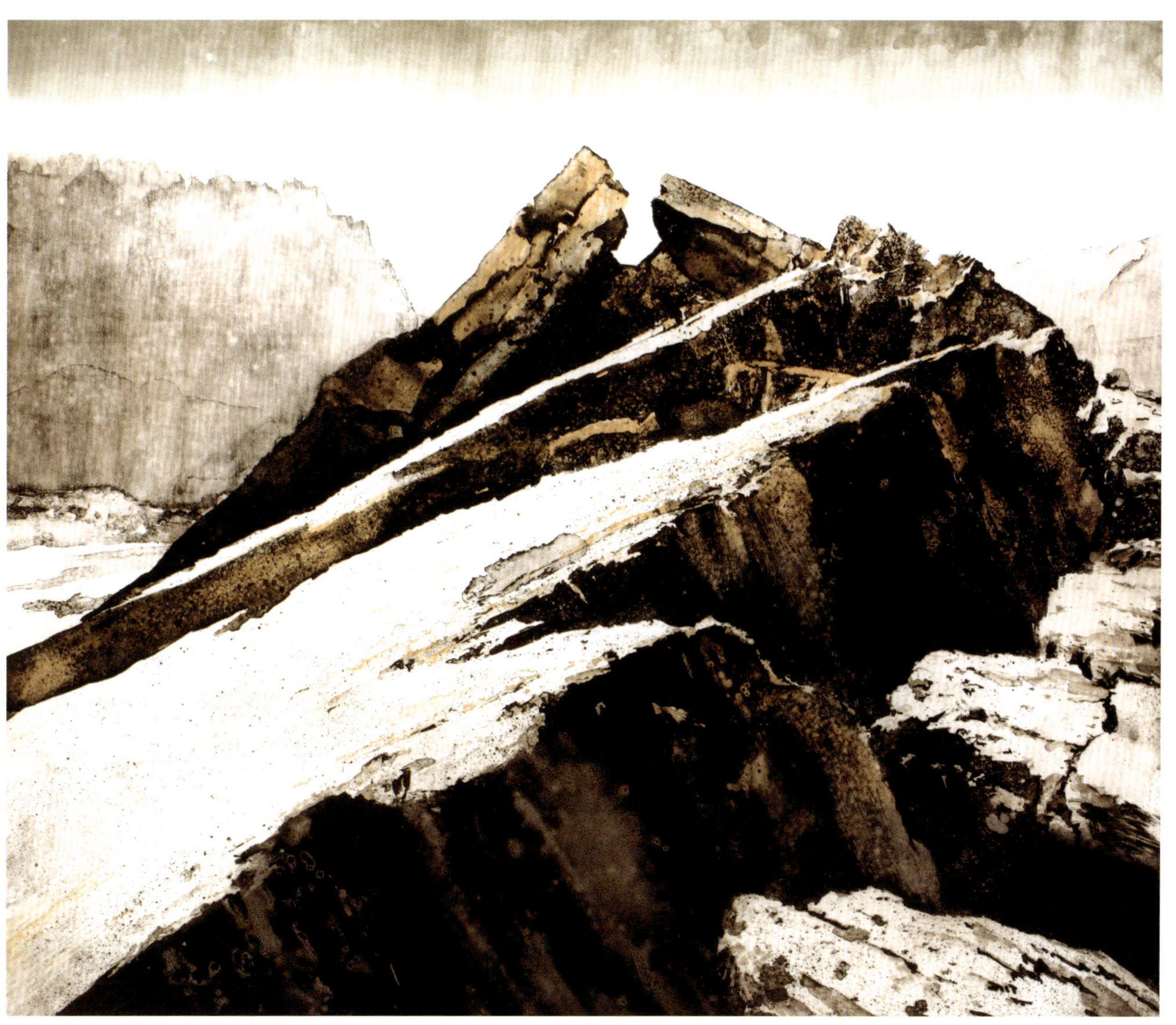

Anthony Whishaw RA RWA
Parched Riverbed

2004-6 · mixed media on canvas · 30 x 45 cm
courtesy the artist · photograph © Roz Woodward

I often experiment with the different effects offered by collage and texture in my work. *Parched Riverbed* uses both techniques to explore the idea of cracked earth and the suggestion of a once-abundant, but now depleted, water source.

By mixing a builders' filler material with acrylic paint, I'm able to create a thick coloured plaster and bring a different physicality to the surface of the canvas, which for this painting brings a tangible sense of gritty realism.

The black and white water motif originated from my observations of raindrops falling into a small puddle outside my studio in the early 2000s, and has subsequently been used in many of my paintings to represent both water as well as tree stumps (when turned by 90 degrees), as in this painting.

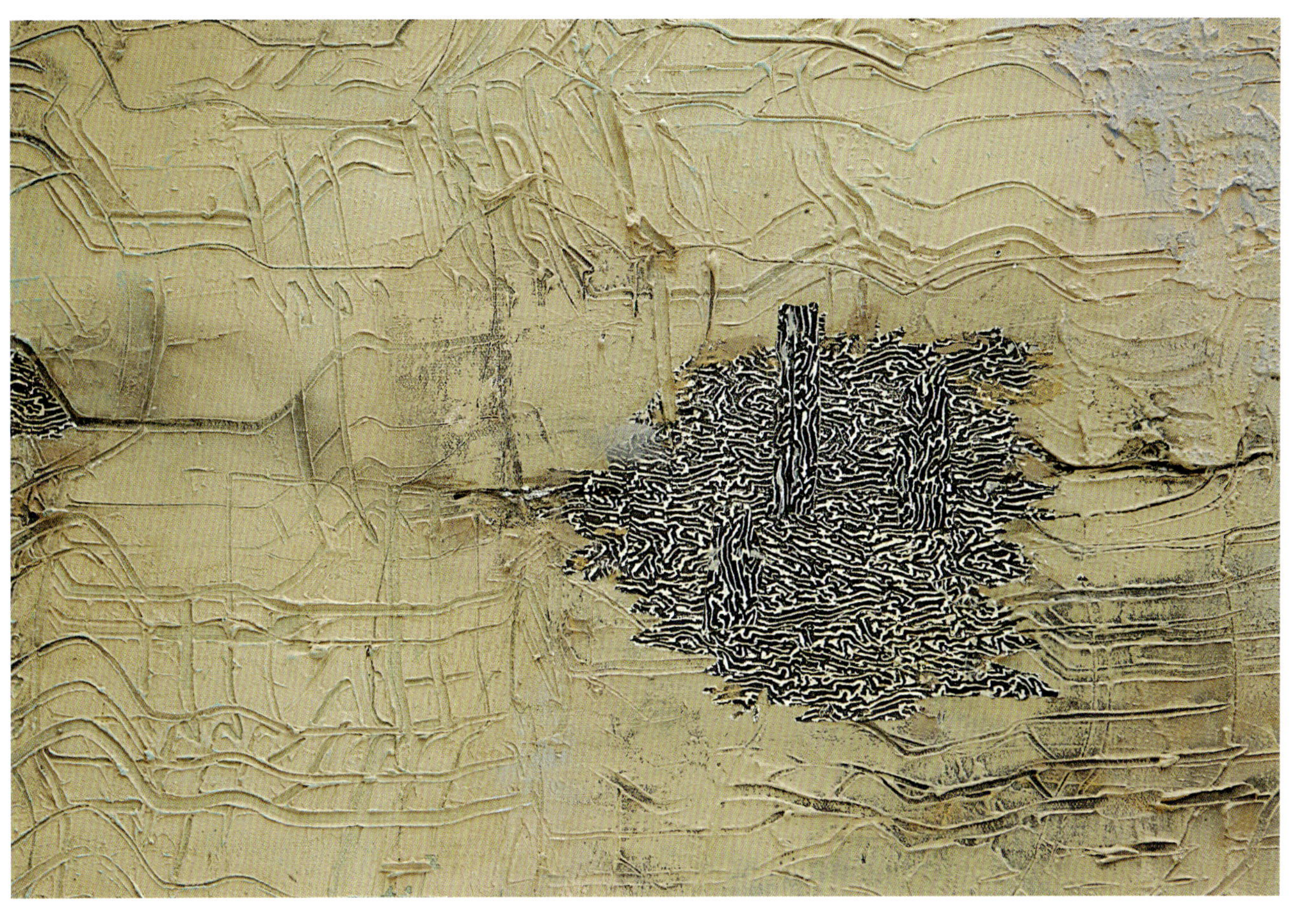

About the artists

Edward Chell
Edward Chell is a London-based artist and Reader in Fine Art at UCA Canterbury. Recent solo projects include the AHRC-funded fellowship and exhibition 'Soft Estate', at Bluecoat, Liverpool, and Spacex, Exeter (2013/14); 'Bloom' at the Horniman Museum and Gardens, London (2015); and 'Common Ground' at Danielle Arnaud Contemporary Art, London (2019). He curated the touring exhibition 'Phytopia' with Glynn Vivian Art Gallery (2019), publishing an accompanying book discussing the wide range of ways that our cultures of plants are visualised and understood.

Alice Cunningham
Alice Cunningham has a diverse practice working with a breadth of materials and is renowned for her sculptural carvings and work in social engagement. She is equally passionate about concept and materiality in her artwork. In 2015, she undertook a residency to carve marble in the quarry that Michelangelo established. Cunningham also had her first solo exhibition that year at the Royal Society of Sculptors, London, and was nominated following year to be on the board of the Society. She was commissioned in 2017 to create a large-scale integrated public artwork in Stoke-on-Trent, dealing with issues surrounding the housing crisis. In 2018, she was selected to represent the UK in a Europe-wide project: her commission was to create a public artwork for the city of Vittorio Veneto, Italy, to commemorate the centenary of the end of the First World War.
www.alicecunningham.co.uk

Dalziel + Scullion RSA
Dalziel + Scullion's studio creates artworks in photography, video, sound and sculpture that explore new artistic languages around the subject of ecology. The work strives to visualise aspects of our shared environment from alternative perspectives and to re-establish and re-evaluate our engagement with the non-human species we live alongside. Matthew Dalziel + Louise Scullion have worked collaboratively for over twenty years. They grew up in Cumnock and Helensburgh respectively, and the differing landscapes they came from, shaped by the activities of mining and defence, have each played an informative part in both their interest in and understanding of landscape. www.dalzielscullion.com

Susan Derges RWA Hon
Susan Derges completed her postgraduate studies at the Slade School of Fine Art before moving to Japan, where she continued her research at Tsukuba University. She is perhaps best known for her pioneering technique of capturing the continuous movement of water by immersing photographic paper directly into rivers or shorelines. Her work has been exhibited in numerous international exhibitions including 'Shadows on the Wall', Museum of Fine Arts, Houston, and 'Shadow Catchers', Victoria and Albert Museum, London. Collections holding her work include J. Paul Getty Museum, Los Angeles; Metropolitan Museum of Art, New York; Victoria and Albert Museum, London. Susan Derges lives and works in Devon.

Anya Gallaccio
Anya Gallaccio lives and works in San Diego, CA, and London, England. She has exhibited widely throughout the world, with institutional solo shows including The Contemporary Austin, Austin, TX (2017); Museum of Contemporary Art San Diego, San Diego, CA (2015); Camden Arts Centre, London, England (2008); Sculpture Center, New York (2006); and Tate Britain, London, England, for the Duveen Sculpture Commission (2002). In 2003 Gallaccio was nominated for the Turner Prize. She is a Professor in the Department of Visual Arts at the University of California, San Diego.

Andrew Hardwick RWA
Andrew Hardwick's work looks at strange wilderness zones, both those seemingly natural and those manmade. He revisits edgeland zones around Bristol's Avonmouth Docks, near where he grew up, and the poetic wilderness of Dartmoor. His paintings are heavily layered with different types of paint, plaster, earth, pigments and other unconventional materials like broken toy cars. They play with ideas of romantic painting and the sublime. Hardwick likes to paint places he knows well. Memory, history and emotion play a large part in his layered elemental artefacts.

Rodney Harris MRSS
Rodney Harris is a sculptor and printmaker who studied for a BA (Hons) Ceramics in Bristol and an MA Ceramics in Cardiff. He has received sculpture commissions from a range of public and private organisations including Peabody London, NHS, Royal Marines, Ibstock Building Products, Liverpool University, Sainsbury's, Bristol City Council and Vale of White Horse District Council. Harris has been a Trustee on the Board of Bristol's Spike Island, a Director of Spike Print Studio, founder of the EarthArt Gallery at Bristol University and is on the Advisory Board for Knowle West Children's Centre, Bristol. His work is in many collections including: Toyaseum (Clay Museum) Incheon, South Korea; Mark Rothko Art Centre, Latvia; Pomona College, California; Eskisehir Municipal Council, Turkey; Liverpool University; and Bristol University. Leverhulme Artist in Residence at Bristol University 2015, Harris also has a long-term collaboration with artist Valda Jackson: Jackson&Harris were winners of the 2017 PSSA Marsh Award for Excellence in Public Sculpture for 'Four Brick Reliefs' in Clapham, London.
www.rodneyharris.co.uk

Fiona Hingston
For twenty years, Fiona Hingston has recorded aspects of her local landscape through drawing, photography and sculpture. She lives and works in a village on the edge of the Mendip Hills and sees her practice as a slow archaeological

enquiry into place and the passage of time. Over the last few years, her observations have become disrupted by the growing awareness of quiet erosion: silent barns, industrial farming methods and vanishing flora and fauna. She sees this local loss as directly connecting to wider issues of commercial standardisation and a diminishing of environmental and cultural diversity. Hingston received an MA in Fine Art Research from the University of the West of England in 2006. She was shortlisted for the Jerwood Drawing Prize in 2008 and 2013 and won the Innovation in Drawing Award at Drawn 2013 at the RWA Bristol. The following year she won the Hauser and Wirth First Prize at the Black Swan Open in Frome, Somerset.

Kabir Hussain

Kabir Hussain studied at Jacob Kramer College in Leeds; Fine Art at South Glamorgan Institute of Higher Education, Cardiff; and for an MA in Sculpture at Chelsea School of Art, London. He is a master founder with over thirty years' experience working in major UK fine art foundries, enabling him to use bronze-casting techniques to explore personal and cultural identity through food and landscape. Kabir approaches his practice in a modular way and creates sculptures according to a theme. His work has been exhibited widely – including the prestigious British Art Show, Hayward Gallery, London (1990); 'Unquiet Moments: Capturing the Everyday', Courtauld Institute of Art, London (2020); and 'Fossilisation: A Slice of the Anthropocene', a solo show at Saffron Walden Museum (2021/22). His work is held in the Arts Council Collection.

Tania Kovats

Tania Kovats studied at Newcastle Polytechnic and the Royal College of Art, London. Notable recent solo exhibitions include 'Head to Mouth', Berwick Gymnasium (2019); 'Troubled Waters', Phoenix Gallery, Exeter (2019); 'Evaporation', Museum of Science and Industry, Manchester (2016); and 'Oceans', Fruitmarket Gallery, Edinburgh (2014). Important recent group exhibitions include 'Un-Natural History' (curated by Invisible Dust), Herbert Museum and Art Gallery, Coventry (2021); 'Future Knowledge', Modern Art Oxford (2018); 'Women Power Protest', Birmingham Museum and Art Gallery (2018); and 'Vita Vitale', Palazzo Grassi, Venice (2015). In 1991 she was awarded the Barclays Young Artist Award at the Serpentine Gallery, London, and in 2015 was nominated for the Max Mara Art Prize for Women at the Whitechapel Gallery. Kovats's work is held in numerous public and private collections including: in London, the Arts Council Collection, British Council, National Maritime Museum, Government Art Collection, Victoria and Albert Museum; Henry Moore Institute, Leeds; Jupiter ArtLand, Edinburgh; Fruitmarket Gallery, Edinburgh; Yale Center for British Art, New Haven, Connecticut; and the Speed Museum, Kentucky. Kovats is currently Professor of Drawing and Making at DJCAD, University of Dundee.

Abigail Lane

Abigail Lane works across a diverse range of mediums, including sculpture, installation, video and photography. She is particularly interested in the uncanny and explores the dark, unsettling aspects of the human psyche, often with a wry, mischievous humour. Lane studied at Goldsmiths College, emerging in the early 1990s alongside artist friends including Mat Collishaw, Sarah Lucas and Gary Hume. She became a key figure in the Young British Artists (YBA) movement and participated in the seminal 1988 'Freeze' exhibition, organised by Damien Hirst with fellow Goldsmiths students. Lane has exhibited extensively across the UK and internationally. In addition to her work as an artist, she curated and co-ordinated SNAP, the contemporary visual art element to Suffolk's Aldeburgh Festival.

Richard Long **CBE RA RWA**

Richard Long makes art about time and distance through the medium of walking. He has made works in the landscapes of all five continents. Since his first exhibition in Düsseldorf in 1968, he has had over 280 solo exhibitions worldwide. Selected exhibitions: Museum of Modern Art, New York (1972); Scottish National Gallery of Modern Art, Edinburgh (1974); Palacio de Cristal, Madrid (1986); Solomon R. Guggenheim Museum, New York (1986); Hayward Gallery, London (1991); National Museum of Modern Art, Kyoto (1996); Tate Britain, London (2009). In 1976, Long represented Britain at the 37th Venice Biennale. Among his honours and awards: the Turner Prize 1989; Chevalier de l'Ordre des Arts et des Lettres from France 1990; Royal Academician 2001; Premium Imperiale in the field of Sculpture from Japan 2009; CBE 2013; Knighthood 2018. Long's works are in many private and public collections.

Siobhán McDonald

Siobhán McDonald is Artist in Residence at the School of Natural Sciences, Trinity College Dublin (2020–23), exploring the Anthropocene and the recent consequences of our treatment of nature. She is working with European cultural Institutions, such as BOZAR: Centre for Fine Arts (Brussels) and Gluon: Platform for Art, Science and Technology (Brussels), on a new project about environmental change. The commissioned artworks will be presented at the Serpentine Gallery, London and Ars Electonica, Austria in 2022. Recent awards include the Arts Council's Project Award 2021; EU Commission Alumni Award 2021; Arts Council's Visual Arts Bursary 2020; Creative Ireland Award 2020; and Climate Whirl Arts Programme Helsinki 2020. Shows in 2022: The Model, Sligo; Centre for Contemporary Art, Laznia, Gdańsk; BOZAR, Brussels; and Centre Culturel Irlandais, Paris. Recent shows include BOZAR, Brussels (2020); Deutsches Hygiene-Museum DHMD, Dresden (2019 and 2020); Volta, Basel (2019); Limerick City Gallery of Art (2019); the National Trust/Fox Talbot Museum, Lacock (2018); Centre Culturel Irlandais, Paris (2018). Her work is represented in many collections, both public and private, such as the Arts Council/An Chomhairle Ealaíon, Allied Irish Banks, Bank of Ireland, the Ulster Museum and Trinity College Dublin. McDonald's projects are supported by the European Commission, the Institute of Physics, Culture Ireland, the Arts Council and the European Research Council.

David Nash OBE RA
Nash has gained an international reputation in a career spanning fifty years with large-scale solo exhibitions of sculptures and drawings all over the world, often featuring site-specific projects. His work is included in numerous group exhibitions and held in prestigious public and private collections worldwide. Working predominantly with wood that becomes available naturally, Nash employs the basic processes of sawing, carving and charring to find meaningful forms. He is also known for initiating long-term 'growing' sculptures and throughout his career has maintained a studio in Blaenau Ffestiniog, north Wales, working with the seasons and elements.

Mariele Neudecker
Mariele Neudecker lives and works in Bristol, UK. In her work, Neudecker is exploring the interphases and overlaps of the two- and three-dimensional, as well as the analogue and digital. She uses a range of media, working with installations, sculpture, video, photography and sound, and has exhibited her work in group and solo exhibitions around Europe and the rest of the world. Neudecker is Professor at Bath School of Art, Film and Media, where she runs the research cluster *Making: Art/Science/Environment*. She works with Pedro Cera, In Camera and Thomas Rehbein Galerie.

Katie Paterson
Katie Paterson is regarded as an artist working at the forefront of her generation. Collaborating with leading scientists and researchers across the world, Paterson's poetic and conceptual projects consider our place on Earth in the context of geological time and change. Her artworks make use of sophisticated technologies and specialist expertise to stage intimate, poetic and philosophical engagements between people and their natural environment. Paterson studied at Edinburgh College of Art and the Slade School of Fine Art. Her work is held in many public collections, both in the UK and internationally, and permanent commissions include *Hollow*, an immersive site-specific work that brings together 10,000 tree species, permanently sited in Royal Fort Gardens, Bristol.

Julian Perry
After studying in Maidenhead and Bristol, Julian Perry has lived and worked in East London for more than thirty years. Perry enjoys an international reputation. His works are held in numerous public and private collections, including that of HRH The Prince of Wales and Bristol Museum and Art Gallery. He has won major British Council and Arts Council England awards and has a varied ongoing exhibition programme. In 2015 his work featured in the Venice Biennale, and in 2022 Southampton City Art Gallery staged the one-person show 'There Rolls the Deep'; he has a forthcoming Artist's Residency at Galloper-Sands gallery, Suffolk.

Michael Porter RWA
Michael Porter studied at Nottingham College of Art (1963–6), Derby College of Art (1967–8) and Chelsea School of Art (1968–72). He worked from his London studio from 1974 until 1997, before moving his studio to Cornwall in 1997. His work has been regularly exhibited in museums and contemporary galleries in London, Europe and America and has been the recipient of numerous major awards such as the National Gallery Artist in Residence, the Lorne Award London University and the Odin Award RWA. Porter received an Honorary Doctorate from Derby University and more recently was made an Honorary Fellow of University College Falmouth. He is represented by Purdy Hicks Gallery. Clive Phillpot: 'He respects the native tradition of landscape painting whilst reinventing it by means of his innovatory techniques and personal vision … his prolific technical experiments have been harnessed to a radical form of realism resulting in works that are equivalent to natural phenomena and which take the viewer into metaphysical realms.'

Kathy Prendergast
Kathy Prendergast is a London-based artist. Her work combines drawing, sculpture and installation and is informed by a range of interests including landscape, mapping, migration, the female body and the relationship between the individual and the wider world. One part of her practice involves painting on topographical maps. She has exhibited widely, most notably at the Venice Biennale 1995, where she won the Premio 2000 for her 'City Drawing' project. Her work is held in many collections both public and private including the Arts Council Collection, the Government Art Collection and Tate Modern.

Carol Rhodes 1959–2018
Carol Rhodes was a Scottish artist, born in Edinburgh. She grew up in Bengal and returned to the United Kingdom at the age of 14 to complete her education. Rhodes studied painting at Glasgow School of Art from 1977 to 1982. After a five-year gap, she resumed painting in 1990 and held her first solo exhibition in 1998. She is known for her paintings of fictional, apparently insignificant, landscapes which are usually viewed from an aerial perspective, making them look almost abstract. Rhodes exhibited internationally and her works are in major collections including Tate, National Galleries of Scotland and the Yale Center for British Art, New Haven, Connecticut. She was diagnosed with Motor Neurone Disease in 2013.

Yinka Shonibare CBE RA
Yinka Shonibare studied Fine Art at Byam Shaw School of Art, London (1989) and received his MFA from Goldsmiths, University of London (1991). His interdisciplinary practice uses citations of Western art history and literature to question the validity of contemporary cultural and national identities within the context of globalisation. Through examining race, class and the construction of cultural identity, his works comment on the tangled interrelationship between Africa and Europe, and their respective economic and political histories.

Anthony Whishaw RA RWA
Anthony Whishaw studied at Chelsea School of Art and the Royal College of Art in London between 1948 and 1955. He was awarded the RCA's travelling scholarship and a Spanish Government Scholarship soon afterwards. His work deals with explorations of memory and experience. On the edge of representation, varying in intent, scale and depiction, his art seeks to reconcile illusion and allusion, the abstract and the figurative. Whishaw has had numerous solo shows throughout the UK and internationally including the Royal Academy of Arts, ICA, Barbican, Kettle's Yard, RWA and in Shanghai, Madrid and Hamburg, among others. He was elected a Royal Academician in 1989 and lives and works in London.

Acknowledgements

The RWA would like to begin by thanking the exhibition's curators and essayists Nathalie Levi, Professor Emerita Christiana Payne and Emma Stibbon RA RWA.

Our sincere thanks to the contemporary artists featured in this book without whom we could not have shown such an exciting range of work, including Edward Chell, Alice Cunningham, Dalziel + Scullion RSA, Susan Derges RWA Hon, Anya Gallaccio, Andrew Hardwick RWA, Rodney Harris MRSS, Fiona Hingston, Kabir Hussain, Tania Kovats, Abigail Lane, Richard Long CBE RA RWA, Siobhán McDonald, David Nash OBE RA, Mariele Neudecker, Katie Paterson, Julian Perry, Michael Porter RWA, Kathy Prendergast, Yinka Shonibare CBE RA, Emma Stibbon RA RWA and Anthony Whishaw RA RWA.

We are equally grateful to the public and private lenders who agreed to loan artwork to the exhibition including Bristol Culture: Bristol Museums & Art Gallery, Courtauld Institute of Art, James Cohan Gallery, Colchester and Ipswich Museum Service, Colchester Borough Council, Ipswich Borough Council, Ingram Art Foundation, Thomas Dane Gallery, Mayor and Commonality and Citizens of the City of London by their Guildhall Art Gallery, Harlow Art Trust c/o Harlow Council, Hull Culture & Leisure Ltd., Ferens Art Gallery: Hull Museums, Hull Culture & Leisure Ltd, Ingleby Gallery, Ipswich Museum Service, Leeds Museums & Galleries (LMG), Leeds City Council, Oxford University Museum of Natural History, Penlee House Gallery & Museum, Purdy Hicks Gallery, Agnés Rein, The Royal Academy of Arts , London, Royal Cornwall Museum, Southampton City Art Gallery, Southampton City Council, Southwark Art Collection, Southwark Council, Tate, Towner Eastbourne, Trustees of the Cecil Higgins Art Gallery (The Higgins Bedford), Trustees of the Imperial War Museum (IWM), University of Brighton, University of Bristol, School of Earth Sciences, Victoria and Albert Museum, City of Wolverhampton Council, Wolverhampton Arts and Culture.

We are also grateful to the many lenders, estates and copyright holders who allowed us to reproduce images in this book. Thanks also to Dr Lorna Linch, University of Brighton. We are of course indebted to Sansom & Co. for their ongoing support, particularly the guidance of Clara Hudson, Ann Kay's editing and Amanda Russell's picture research.

Our thanks go to Arts Council England for an Arts Council National Lottery Project Grant that supported engagement and outreach activity related to the exhibition along with funding for new commissions by Richard Long and Alice Cunningham.

The exhibition has been made possible as a result of the Government Indemnity Scheme. The RWA would like to thank HM Government for providing Government Indemnity and the Department for Digital, Culture, Media and Sport and Arts Council England for arranging the indemnity.

Finally we would like to thank all the staff and volunteers at the RWA who have helped make this book and the exhibition possible, in particular Lois Clark, Kate Foster, Helen Jacobs and Sooz Moon.

About the authors

Nathalie Levi is Head of Programme and Curator of Exhibitions at the RWA, Bristol. She specialises in exhibitions that bridge the contemporary and historic, with a focus on twentieth-century British art. Selected past exhibition curation, co-curation and production include 'Refuge and Renewal: Migration and British Art' (RWA, 2020), 'Furious, Wild and Young: The Death of Chatterton' (RWA, 2020), 'Albert Irvin and Abstract Expressionism' (RWA, 2019), 'Togetherness: Contemporary Art Collaborations' (RWA, 2018), 'Sawdust and Sequins: The Art of the Circus' (RWA, 2018), 'Kenneth Armitage: Sculpture and Drawing of the 1950s' (The Stanley & Audrey Burton Gallery, University of Leeds, 2017), 'György Gordon 1924–2005: A Retrospective' (The Stanley & Audrey Burton Gallery, 2016) and 'Buying Time': Part One: David Lisser, Part Two: Graham Dolphin and Part Three: Zoe Walker and Neil Bromwich (Northern Gallery for Contemporary Art, Sunderland, 2013–14). She is a recipient of the British Council and ICOM UK Global Travel Grant and has an MFA in Curating from Goldsmiths, University of London and a BA (Hons) in Fine Art from Newcastle University.

Christiana Payne is Professor Emerita of History of Art at Oxford Brookes University. She has published widely on British art of the eighteenth and nineteenth centuries. Her books include *Toil and Plenty: Images of the Agricultural Landscape in England 1780–1890* (Yale University Press, 1993), *Where the Sea Meets the Land: Artists on the Coast in Nineteenth-century Britain* (Sansom & Co., 2007), *John Brett: Pre-Raphaelite Landscape Painter* (Yale University Press, 2010) and *Silent Witnesses: Trees in British Art 1760–1870* (Sansom & Co., 2017). Exhibitions that she has curated or co-curated include 'Objects of Affection: Pre-Raphaelite Portraits by John Brett' (Barber Institute of Fine Arts, University of Birmingham, 2010), 'A Walk in the Woods: A Celebration of Trees in British Art' (The Higgins Bedford, 2017–18) and 'Pre-Raphaelites: Drawings and Watercolours' (Ashmolean Museum, Oxford, 2021). At the RWA, she has co-curated three recent exhibitions: 'The Power of the Sea: Making Waves in British Art 1790–2014', 'Air: Visualising the Invisible in British Art 1768–2017' and 'Fire: Flashes to Ashes in British Art 1692–2019'.

Emma Stibbon **RA RWA** is an artist working in drawing and print, and is Senior Lecturer at the University of Brighton. Her work depicts environments that are undergoing dynamic change. She has taken part in several international residencies, including the Arctic Circle.org (2022); Queen Sonja Print Award Residency in Svalbard (2019); Death Valley National Park Artist-in-Residence (2019); Artist-in-Residence at Hawaiʻi Volcanoes National Park (2016); Artist-in-Residence Josef & Anni Albers Foundation, Connecticut (2016); and Artist Placement in Antarctica, Scott Polar Research Institute (2013). Stibbon shows her work widely, including the solo exhibitions 'Fire and Ice' (Cristea Roberts Gallery, London, 2019), 'Territories of Print 1994–2019' (Rabley Drawing Centre, Marlborough, 2019), 'Broken Ground' (Galerie Bastian, Berlin, 2017) and 'Ice Limit' (The Polar Museum, University of Cambridge, 2015). She also exhibited work commissioned for 'Ruskin, Turner & the Storm Cloud' (York Art Gallery and Abbot Hall, Kendal, 2019). Her work is held in private and public collections, including the Stadtmuseum, Berlin; Potsdam Museum; Laing Art Gallery, Newcastle upon Tyne; The New Art Gallery, Walsall; Pallant House Gallery, Chichester; The Polar Museum, University of Cambridge; Bristol Museum & Art Gallery; Russell-Cotes Art Gallery, Bournemouth; the Fitzwilliam Museum, Cambridge; and the Victoria and Albert Museum, London. In 2013 she was elected Royal Academician and in 2018 was awarded Honorary Doctor of Letters by the University of Bristol.